The Spirit Of Spain

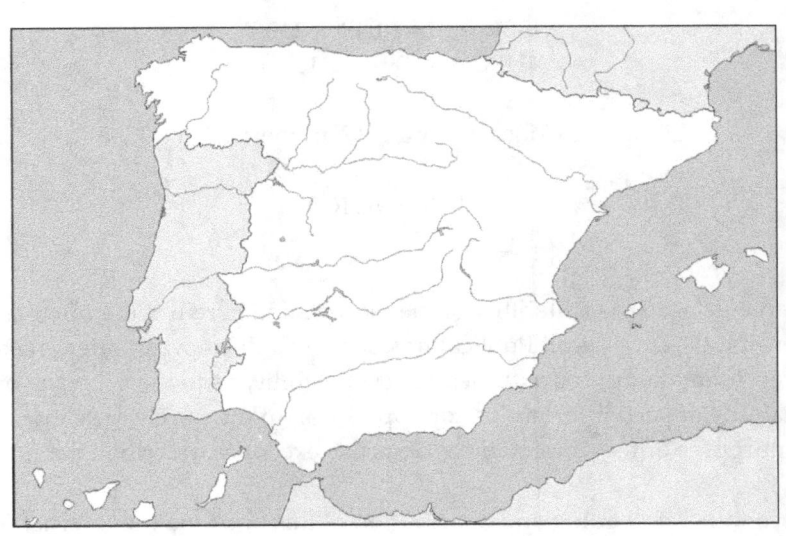

HAROLD RALEY

TotalRecall Publications, Inc.
1103 Middlecreek
Friendswood, TX 77546
281-992-3131 TEL
www.totalrecallpress.com

All rights reserved. Except as permitted under the United States Copyright Act of 1976, No part of this publication may be reproduced, stored in a retrieval system, or transmitted in any form or by any means electronic or mechanical or by photocopying, recording, or otherwise without prior permission of the publisher. Exclusive worldwide content publication / distribution by TotalRecall Publications, Inc.

Copyright © 2023 by: Harold Raley

ISBN: 978-1-64883-313-7
UPC: 6-43977-63137-4

Library of Congress Control Number: 2023937587

FIRST EDITION
1   2   3   4   5   6   7   8   9   10

Judgments as to the suitability of the information herein is the purchaser's responsibility. TotalRecall Publications, Inc. extends no warranties, makes no representations, and assumes no responsibility as to the accuracy or suitability of such information for application to the purchaser's intended purposes or for consequences of its use except as described herein.

The scanning, uploading and distribution of this book via the Internet or via any other means without the permission of the publisher is illegal and punishable by law. Please purchase only authorized electronic editions and do not participate in or encourage electronic piracy of copyrighted materials. Your support of the author's rights is appreciated.

To Julián Marías
In gratitude and admiration

CONTENTS

Introduction i

Chapter 1: The Presence of Spain 1
    A. "Romantic" Spain 1
    B. The Presence of Spain 3

Chapter 2 Spain In The Light Of Its History 10
    A "Phenomenology" of Spanish History 10
    B. What is Spain? 15
    C. Spanish Origins 21
    D. The Theme of 'Spanish "Decadence" 26
    E. Modern Revisionism 29
    F The Inquisition and the Indies 32
    G. The Spanish "Colonial" System 38
    H. Errors of Interpretation 43
    I. Al-Andalus and Spain 45

Chapter 3: Spain and Europe 53
    A. Inventing the Future 53
    B. The Duality of Spanish Futurism. 59
    C. Reinterpreting the Renaissance? 62
    D. The Hebrew Vision of the Future 67
    E. Implications of the Christian World View 69
    F Europe and the West 77
    G. Forms of 'Nationalism and Patriotism 79
    H. Spain and the Modern Mind 85
    I. Ideas and Belief 92
    J. Protestantism and the Modern Perspective 97
    K. Conflicting Theories of Human Life 101
    L. After Retrenchment 110

Chapter 4: Beyond Modernity the Generations of 1898 113
    A. The Quest: The First Generation of 1898..113
    B. Theoretical Orientation: The Second Generation. 131
    C. Artistic Assimilation: The Third Generation 144
    D. Consolidation: The Fourth Generation 152

Chapter 5: The Spirit of Spain 158
    A. Spanish "Stoicism"?..158
    B. Comparative Spiritual Registers...163
    C. Literary Constants..168
    D. Master Tropes: Spain and Don Quixote...175
    E. Quixotic life and the Western Mind..183
    F Whither España ? 196

Notes 203
    Chapter I..203
    Chapter2 207
    Chapter 3 211
    Chapter 5 213

Bibliography 215

Introduction

For centuries Spain has been a country foreigners love to hate and Spaniards hate to love. Yet visitors swarm to it by the millions, seduced by the very things they publicly decry. It may be the most visited and most reviled country in modern times. Few nations have been more studied and probably none more persistently misunderstood.

My personal introduction to Spain was also paradoxical. From my earliest university days several of my professors taught me that Spain was a land known for glorious beginnings and inglorious endings. To hear them tell it, it was an embarrassment to modernity, a country done in by religious fanaticisms and medieval backwardness.

But the more I listened to these gloomy assessments of Spain, the more this strange country attracted me. In my commonsense ignorance I asked these teachers why they bothered with a civilization they found so deficient. They responded to my naïve questions by telling me that the Hispanic world is huge and that the Spanish language is culturally and commercially important; and, second, that Spanish and Hispanic literatures are worth studying despite creative gaps and eras of mediocrity.

I was unconvinced by these truisms. By explaining everything they explained nothing. My personal imperative then became clear: I had to discover for myself the key to this mysterious Spanish Spirit. In one form or another the task would run like a thread through my life. Not that the work is complete. Far from it; I have learned only enough to realize how much I do not, nor likely ever will, know completely.

For the reasons alluded to above, the views that I shall express in this book did not develop in simple linear stages. That might have been true had my starting point been one of simple ignorance about Spain and the Hispanic world. But that was not the case. From the first I learned many things about Spain; the problem was that many of them later proved false or else were cast in a false context that distorted their meaning.

Intellectual honesty obliged me, then, to return to the most basic assumptions, to reexamine and justify anew nearly everything I had learned about Spain. There were moments of confusion as my earlier bookish facts crumbled one by one under closer scrutiny and visits to Spain itself. But there was a gain in this loss. Finally free of old clichés, I was ready to see Spain with my own eyes.

The problem now took a different slant. I faced the moral obligation of trying to justify at each stage the new directions I took. It proved to be a lasting injunction; this urgency to see things for myself and rethink them in ways I could personally absorb has always acted at the core of my Iberian meditations, more, has generally determined and justified their course. Perhaps this is why I took so readily and naturally to the ancient Spanish intuition that knowledge must be lived in order to be truly real.

I asked myself the same question I had put to my teachers many years earlier: why should I devote so much time to Spain? Was it misdirected curiosity on my part, as some have objected to me, or are there more transcendent issues at stake? This book is a response to these questions.

There were problems with this posture. Though not an "expert" on Spain, I knew enough about Spanish studies to realize that most professional hispanists would reject my theses. (I remind myself constantly that contemporary hispanism often has very little to do with Spain.) Yet even though my views were unpopular, unlike Aladdin's mother, I was never tempted to exchange what I believed to be the magic lamp of truth for fashionable but false substitutes.

It would be impossible to acknowledge all the debts I have accumulated in the making of this book. Impressionistic scenes from Hispanic cities and natural panoramas, lasting friendships and passing acquaintances with Spaniards of every condition, travels in several lands and further journeys through many books, all these memories crowd about me now and clamor for their place in this writing. I cannot do them justice. The best I can manage here is to say that I alone am responsible for any errors or distortions their image may suffer.

Chapter 1:
The Presence of Spain

A. *"ROMANTIC" SPAIN*

James Michener begins his admirable book <u>Iberia</u> with the opinion that sooner or later every person of romantic or mystical leanings must come to grips with Spain. Many foreign artists have found inspiration in this vision of Spain as a romantic, mystical country. In <u>Childe Harold</u>, for example, Byron gushed over Spain in this conventionally romantic manner:

Oh, lovely Spain! renown'd romantic land!

Nor would I dispute Michener, Byron, Washington Irving, Victor Hugo, Stendhal, or other writers and artists who took Spain to be a quintessentially romantic land. The Spain they described exists, or has existed, at least insofar as they have molded it into a fictional reality. I would only add that for me their view falls short. For as I see it, not only the romantic and the mystic but also all persons of Western roots must take Spain seriously if they would discover their deepest reality and care to learn who they really are. This book is my attempt to explain why this is so.

Regardless of the fascination they may hold for us, some countries remain decidedly foreign to us. Though odd in many ways, Spain is not among them. Many fundamental aspects of our Western life, long since stricken from our common cultural patrimony, survive in Spain and in her offspring civilizations, even though this legacy is often misunderstood and scorned. This is why for Western peoples the Spanish way of life, "...that simple Spanish vibration in the face of chaos," as Ortega once described it, far from being an excursion into an exotic, alien world, often leads to the discovery of things that resonate to their own spiritual cadence. For the experience of Spain reminds them of their original Western heritage, as a familiar melody stirs our poignant memories of cherished bygone times.

Hence the curious experience of recognizing ourselves in Spanish culture. As though rediscovering certain essential icons of our life forgotten or suppressed for centuries in our native circumstance, on Spanish soil we see these inchoate images begin to take on form and retrieve their original meaning. We have the exhilarating sensation of living in these crucial, momentary junctures not an ersatz Spanish life—for we ourselves are not and cannot be Spaniards—but our own life in ways that have either vanished entirely or subsist in mutilated form in our own lands. Thus, we often experience in Spanish life that unique and paradoxical vital plenitude that has forever transcended and rendered secondary its very real and undeniable material limitations and inconveniences.

This discovery usually accompanies another. We come to see also that the true romanticism of Spain has never consisted in mere escapism, not in an ethereal flight from real life, as the Northern Romantics urged, but in an irresistible movement toward it, as the enlightened thinkers of Spain's own Generation(s) of 1898 described so eloquently. Unlike the ideal loves that nourish conventional romanticism, an abiding passion for the real-world fuels Spain's "reverse romanticism." For the Spanish have always respected reality above all else in this life, convinced as they are that taken without apology and with its full complement of pains and shortcomings, but also with its delights and promises, this world still exceeds by far all its charming, ideal counterfeits.

This distinction is not really so neat and straightforward as it may first seem. For as we shall see later, within the Spanish context what we commonly think of as the "real world" acquires certain additional dimensions that not only set it apart from other conceptions of the real but also may hamper our understanding of the Spanish mind.

Partly because of Spanish resistance to what I shall call the "substitutionary forms" of modern idealism, there arose a view of Spain as an anachronistic country and the antithesis of enlightened modernity. I shall have more to say later on this topic, yet I see no reason not to admit here that the accusation contains a certain truth. The only question here is whether the anachronism is backward or forward. For we must ask whether Spain simply jumped track in modern times, as a great many of her own thinkers claim, or whether the traits that caused her to deviate from modernity are the same ones that could serve her well in a future world, as Havelock Ellis once suggested.

B. THE PRESENCE OF SPAIN

As early as the Enlightenment, modernity delivered its unfavorable verdict against Spain, but now as the modern world flounders amid postmodern cant and its moral and philosophical certitudes peter out in extremist absurdities, that sentence begins to appear both hasty and haughty.

But while the uniqueness of Spanish history may hold its own against today's declining modernist minimalism, where does it stand in regard to the current "globalist" tendency to disregard the deep structures of history, in effect to question the very notion of history itself? For over against the view that the lives of nations, like persons, have an individual plot or "argument"—a "history" in the original meaning of the term—that distinguishes them from others and only needs a proper telling to be understood, as Ortega claimed, there stands the opposing assumption that this "narrative" or "historical" understanding must give way to data-driven conclusions and statistical profiles.

It seems to me that part of the confusion can be traced to the fact that some countries do indeed coincide essentially with this superficial pattern. Those of recent creation lack historical roots, in some cases, even historical justification, and this means that their reality consists for the most part in their surface appearances.

Others countries, and among them Spain, can by no means be confined to this bare image. As Heidegger once remarked, the Spanish are a people who have commanded in the world. Their "presence" includes, at a minimum, not only who they are but also the aura of who they have been and what they have meant historically. Nor is Spain unique in its multileveled reality. In a similar way, we can speak of "lesser" and "greater" France. Other nations often fought the former—think of the Napoleonic era—while succumbing to the cultural grandeur of the latter. Much the same could be said of Great Britain, which preserved its introverted "island" eccentricity even as it grew into a world empire. In our day, the United States naturally answers to its people, sometimes in jingoistic terms, but under its greater image and alternate name "America" it belongs also to the world.

Naturally these comparative comments do not resolve the

problem of Spanish history. At bottom we discover that we have entered into an implicit epistemological debate on what constitutes human and historical knowledge in the first place. For according to the first premise, countries—like individuals—can be understood only in the light of what they strive to become—successfully or unsuccessfully—in time and over time; whereas to take the second view is to presuppose that they cannot, nor need not, transcend what they are at the moment and, consequently, that historical projection and purpose are essentially irrelevant to understanding. The first assumption centers on the immeasurable factor of human resourcefulness, while the second concentrates on quantifiable material resources. It is sobering to realize that had the second view prevailed in Classical times, the "greatness that was Greece" would have been a mere footnote of history.

Not by accident we owe primarily to twentieth-century Spanish thinkers the great corrective discovery that human reality cannot properly be understood by non-human references and conceptual instruments coded for the manipulation of physical or biological reality. This was the prime assumption of modernity; this also was its great debacle.

I repeat that this was not by chance, for whenever we penetrate beyond modernist cant and approach the heart of human matters, we discover to our surprise, as did Michener and countless others who have yielded to its fascination, that Spain is strangely central to the humanistic endeavor. But our surprise diminishes as we probe deeper and discover that the twin streams that have always nourished Western life, its Classical and Christian heritages, flow deepest in this ancient land.

This is why despite its marginal political and economic

weight—the standard barometers of greatness in our time—Spain continues to be intensely present and important in the world in a wholly different sense that we shall examine in later chapters. Indeed, it will be the informing premise of this book.

I do not mean to leave the impression that historically Spain has lived up to some high measure of human perfection unmatched by neighboring peoples. Well-meaning apologists have sometimes claimed as much and have done considerable harm to the image of Spain as a result. As I see it, the age-old "problem" of Spain devolves on this paradoxical dilemma: historically the Spanish have sensed that they failed to live up to a superior ideal even as other Europeans efficiently lived down to what the Spanish believed to be an inferior one. Few countries have customarily dwelt so far below their true calling as Spain, and few, if any, have suffered more remorse because of it. In time the modern bourgeois world made its inroads in Spanish life, but its material comforts could not compensate Spaniards for compromising their high calling. For the Spanish, Quixotic at their core, low success cannot atone for their superior failure. And precisely because of their almost neurasthenic sense of moral shortcomings, Spaniards have tended to be extraordinarily harsh with themselves, a trait lately conspicuous in certain other countries as well. Perhaps this is why until recent years they were more likely to describe their collective dilemmas in terms of national sin and redemption than in the customary modern concepts of politics and economics.

It remains to be seen whether the recent conversion of Spanish intellectuals to the statistical methods and value-neutral concepts of their Western counterparts will turn out to be more apparent than genuine. Later I shall have more to say on this. It is important for those subsequent considerations, however, to introduce this premise: just as a fair understanding of Spain's achievements requires a direct reference to its enduring national aspirations, so its internally perceived failures must be judged in the light of historical Spanish trajectories. And we must add this: perhaps the greatest obstacle to appreciating what Spain is has been the failure to understand what Spain believed it could have been—and should have been—and was not.

To hear many Spaniards tell it, their national history has been a long, disheartening litany of errors. To which the modern world nods in general agreement. This theme deserves further treatment, but for the moment let us simply accept the kernel of truth it contains, taking time to add something I believe to be essential. Throughout their long history the Spanish have made more than their share of mistakes, as their enemies claim. But this will mislead us unless we bear in mind that, generally speaking, their errors were not about the secondary, remediable problems common to other countries but instead had to do with the most fundamental things, those that really count in individual life. Yet as paradoxical as it may sound, far from being an accusation, this is really an indication that they have remained relatively close to the truth. For instance, while Enlightenment intellectuals of other nations were embracing varieties of the "modern substitutionary idealism" I spoke of earlier with its false solutions to real problems, the Spanish continued to raise—often in inadequate ways—the basic questions about human destiny. To put it another way, the Spanish stayed close enough to the truth to make truthful mistakes. This despite the fact that for long periods of its history formal, academic philosophy of the European mold languished in Spanish universities. We must look elsewhere—in art, literature, religion, and popular life—for the elements of a genuine Spanish metaphysics. For Spain produced nothing resembling modern Cartesianism; it had no Bacon, Leibniz, or Kant, no Nietzsche or Newton, but it had Cervantes, Saint Teresa, Saint John of the Cross, Gracián, Velázquez, Calderón, and Goya to portray in dramatic human terms its surprisingly coherent vision of the world. The sudden appearance of a mature Spanish philosophy in the early twentieth century may be taken as evidence of the vigor of its subterranean roots.

It is perfectly valid and proper, of course, to question or even disagree with the responses provided by the Spanish way of thinking, for this is how authentic thought renews itself, but above all it is necessary to respect the questions themselves from which the Spanish thinkers and metaphysicians would not be dislodged, for this is how authentic thought revives from age to age. No wonder, then, that as other Westerners reject minimalism and scale again the peaks of authentic thought, they find the Spanish thinkers awaiting them at the summits.

There are times when we must agree with the Duke of Wellington who remarked, "How difficult it is to understand the Spanish exactly." Or again, "Spain is the only country where two and two do not make four." In his exasperation the Iron Duke made a point but probably missed a more telling one. While the Spanish know that logic works as well in Spain as anywhere else, they have never found a compelling reason to conform their lives to this small fact.

Because it is so intense, Spanish reality far exceeds its modest statistical profile. How, then, do we begin taking measure of something so elusive as the "Spanish spirit"? Perhaps by reminding ourselves that we are dealing with human reality and that, as Ortega y Gasset claimed, in order to understand anything truly human we must tell a story. But there is a further truth to keep in mind: the story of Spain is not an impersonal tale or a matter of idle curiosity. As the poet Horace said long ago, *Nomine mutato, de te fabula narratur,* change the name and the story is about you.

Chapter 2
Spain In The Light Of Its History

A "Phenomenology" of Spanish History

By a "phenomenology" of Spanish history I have in mind not an examination of what might be called, according to classical Husserlian terminology, its "phenomenological objects"—crises, conflicts, wars, heroes, dynasties, etc. —but rather the unique mode in which these and other historical elements generally have been perceived by Spaniards. In other words, I am interested primarily in the peculiar and characteristic perspectives within and from which Spanish history has appeared, appealed, disturbed, and persisted over time. This is, or so I believe, the surest—if not the shortest—way toward an understanding of the Spanish spirit. An example may help illustrate my point.

Before their zeal of recent years to imitate other countries, the Spanish were often criticized for neglecting the monuments of their history, and for the most part this attitude was held up as evidence of a disturbing indifference toward their past. No doubt this was true in many individual cases, yet under closer scrutiny this apparent unconcern appears to be not a matter of indifference but instead a function of a stubborn Spanish resistance to obsolescence. As a result, even though Spain is full of chronologically old things, few of them are truly antique and merely "monumental" or "historical" relics. Curiously enough, some of the "monuments" that foreign visitors take to be the quintessential markers of Spanish history—the Alhambra, for instance—really are admirable relics that have failed the test of this functional continuity. Perhaps this misunderstanding ought not to surprise us. Unamuno once remarked that foreigners take from Spain only what clashes least with their spirit and best suits the image they already have of it, an idea that is always and necessarily superficial.

Traditionally, in Spain things—and people—seem to resist with extraordinary resiliency the early end of their place and purpose. For this reason, far from being merely a nostalgic indulgence in historical symbolism in, say, the British or American style, this continuity consists instead of a vigorous and normal participation in everyday life. No doubt this is why the old and the elderly are treated not with the fawning deference that other societies show toward quaint survivors of earlier times, but the natural respect earned by functional reality. Perhaps this partially accounts for the exceptional human vitality and cultural depths of a land not often politically fortunate and only modestly endowed with natural resources.

It would be a mistake, however, to think this human acceptance applies only to living persons. Physical death does not necessarily eradicate their personal or cultural presence. The fate of certain noted writers, for example, is illuminating. Take the case of Unamuno who died in 1936. He continues to be present—as he prophesied he would—in an entirely different sense, for Spaniards continue to read his books and—to an unusual degree—keep his personality alive. The same could be said for other members of his generation—Azorín and Baroja, for instance—and even for earlier Spaniards such as Galdós.

This lingering "presence" of the departed and the prestige they retain long after their death give Spanish culture a human depth and complexity probably unmatched today in other Western societies.[1] In many so-called "modern" cultures death—and often the old age that precedes it—disqualifies the elderly and the deceased and erases at once from the public mind the legitimacy of their ideas and the esteem they once enjoyed.

This vital retention of the past means that the Spanish have traditionally lived a more inclusive "present time" than many other modern societies and in this regard preserve a feature of life that has weakened elsewhere. In other eras the "present" was a relatively broad band of time that included considerable portions of the past and fluctuating amounts of the foreseeable future. In contrast, the modern "present" is characterized by temporal narrowness. "Now," or "right now," tends to replace what we used to call "the present time." And even as this reduction was occurring, modern people were amassing, like travelers cluttered with excessive baggage, more projects and tasks than their ever-shrinking band of "present time" could possibly accommodate.

Because of this deep commitment to human continuity, what Unamuno with admirable insight would come to call "intrahistory," **the Spanish have understood and lived their history not as something they have but as something they are.** Customarily they are inclined to see their history not as what died but what survives and lives on as the substance—and often the tragedy—of their life and country. Consequently, the proper starting point for understanding Spanish history is not some temporal point in the past but the human situation in the present.

No wonder, then, the Spanish have refused to confine their history to museums, chronicles, and monuments. Unlike other nations, they have always known in one way or another that history does not have to be written to be real.

But by that same reasoning it is real only insofar as it is living reality. For this reason. to the degree that their history has been restricted to history books, the Spanish have sensed its reductionism and complained about its distortion. Because they fail to account for the real historical depth and significance of Spain, these official versions of their history have at once interested them least and troubled them most. Left to their native disposition, they have preferred intuitively to express their living history in the marketplace and the plaza and in what the poet Milton called "the busy hum of men."

There appear to be at least three major inherent dangers in taking this view of history. The first is a predisposition toward historical determinism, that is, the assumption that the past predetermines the present, and since the past as such is unchangeable in the usual sense, then its predominance is unappealable.

When taken to an extreme, this collapses further into simple fatalism, which in its popular forms, centers on the conviction that the good in life is brief and exceptional and that only the ills we endure can be counted on. Ultimately the fatalist counts only on evil and calamity. If, therefore, the Spanish **are** their history and not merely its heirs or owners, as other nations are more prone to believe, then its deficiencies must be taken very much to heart, for they are also personal and national shortcomings. We shall see, for instance, how this dialectical association was especially evident in the first "generations" of 1898 who betrayed in their attitudes the assumption that the collective problems of Spanish society were inescapably the imperfect substance of their own lives.

The second problem is the other extreme. If Spanish history with all its perceived imperfections translates directly into an unwholesome and burdensome personal and public life, then one way to shed its onus is to disqualify it altogether and by rejecting it, to begin anew. This radical idealism run amok was evident as early as Father Bartolomé de Las Casas whose <u>Brevíssima historia de la destruyción de las Indias</u> (1552) helped to establish the myth of "destructive" Spain and to instill in the nations of Hispanic descent the gloomy suspicion that they are genetically flawed because of their cultural ancestry. This despite the fact, as Menéndez Pidal points out, that Spain was the only nation seriously concerned with the survival of native peoples (<u>El Padre las Casas</u>, p. 386). The "revolutionary" tradition of much of Latin America—"Marxist" Cuba for example—owes much to this vituperation of the Hispanic legacy.

In opposition to these positions there arises yet another view with its own extremist features. I refer to the counter tendency not to condemn Spain unilaterally for its alleged failures but to praise it uncritically for its supposed superior virtues. To a certain degree, this is a normal reaction to the disqualification of Spain mentioned above. Obviously, the country that has been the greatest builder since Rome and the motherland of sublime art and letters cannot be merely the depraved society its harshest critics accuse it of being. On the other hand, to exaggerate truth is always to diminish it. Although he acted with loftier aims, the scholarly Menéndez Pelayo made exorbitant claims in favor of Spain that reveal an odd polemical kinship with the bitter tirades of others such as novelist Juan Goytisolo against it.

The prime imperative of any phenomenological understanding is fidelity to reality. For just as things have the inherent right to reveal themselves on their own terms without preconditions or substitutions, so we have the moral and intellectual obligation to respect that right. This means that Spain deserves to be seen in the light of its own history, not in the radiance of other nations.

Yet in the three centuries between Father Mariana's <u>Historia general de España</u> (1601) and the rise of the generations of 1898 this prime imperative was usually ignored. For three hundred years rival nations controlled the canon of Spanish history, passing damaging judgement on what they saw as its scant achievements and many shortcomings. Small wonder, then, that during the whole modern era Spain came to be looked upon within and without as an eccentric country that generally defied the norms and rejected the advances of modern Europe. But as we shall see, this is not the whole story.

B. WHAT IS SPAIN?

Ortega asked the fundamental question of his age, "My God, what is Spain? His query was to reverberate throughout twentieth-century Spanish thought. As late as 1970, for example, Laín Entralgo would entitle one of his books <u>¿A qué llamamos España?</u> (What is This That We Call Spain?). The question persists because it points to the paradox of modern Spanish history. For after having repelled Islamic expansionism in Iberia and the Mediterranean basin, after having created the first modern state with its new military and diplomatic structures, and after having discovered, or better, invented, the Americas, Spain pulled back, withdrew from the rest of Europe, and seemed thereafter to be unable or unwilling to live at the level of the very civilization she had made possible. Pondering this enigma noted historian Stanley Payne comments: "It is not easy... to explain why a country that showed such energy, enterprise, and even organizational ability in the sixteenth century should in more recent times have found it impossible to achieve national unity and institutional cohesion."[2] As María Zambrano notes, "It was the West in its science and its philosophy that really stood to gain from these quintessentially Spanish discoveries."[3]

At the same time, even as twentieth-century Spanish thinkers took note of this oddity, they anguished over the equally anomalous contrast between the obvious depth and richness of Spanish history and the superficiality and negligible impact of Spain's political and institutional presence in the modern world.

This contrast led some, among them Unamuno, to speak of "two" Spains: popular and profound Spain, which he called "intrahistorical," and its political and superficial alter ego that he termed official and "historical." From our viewpoint, the evidence for such a dichotomy is weak. Instead, it seems more reasonable to argue that there has always been a single Spain that at certain moments has been poorly understood and, therefore, poorly lived because it has been taken to be something it was not. Here let me advance the premise that over the centuries a certain falsified view has caused a series of disturbances and prejudiced the understanding of Spain. But though falsified, this understanding is not wholly false. In order to understand it, we shall have to return to the reality and the conditions that gave rise to it. For if the notion of "two" Spains is a falsification, it had to be of something that was not originally and totally false.

Some countries know very well "who" they are. For them Ortega's plea would simply be a melodramatic exaggeration. France, for instance, like all countries with a long history, has had its low moments and French critics have not ceased to point out their nation's shortcomings and missteps. Yet as far as I know, the French have never seriously questioned their French condition itself. As early as <u>La Chanson de Roland</u> in references made in deliciously archaic French to *"La doulce France"* we can sense the satisfying commitment to being French. And limiting our comments to those countries that have been leaders in the world, the same could be said of "Merrye olde England."

For other countries, however, and among them Spain, their very condition often seems problematic. If, as we have seen, foreign intellectuals and artists frequently insisted on translating Spanish reality into romantic and picturesque motifs, the Spanish themselves knew better even if they did not always know clearly who they were.

This brings us to yet another paradox of modern Spain, one that has often been noted but perhaps never explained on its own terms. 1 refer to the sensation often experienced by the Spanish, and many times attributed to mere arrogance, of being vitally and personally already beyond or above the range of modern rationalism at the moment of receiving it. For his part, Unamuno summarized this Spanish viewpoint by stating that Saint Teresa was worth any European institution and any Kantian <u>Critique of Pure Reason</u>.[4] In a similar vein, Ortega would say that as a student of philosophy in Germany he found respected professors, chairs, courses, universities, and great philosophic traditions, indeed everything but creative philosophy. He went on to observe that whereas institutionally there was no question of the superiority of other European nations, the same could hardly be said about individual intellectuals whom he often found to be less impressive than their Spanish counterparts.

In passing, we need to be aware that for better or worse during those periods when Spain was most open to European trends—most of the eighteenth century, the second half of the nineteenth and the first decades of the twentieth—philosophic creativity had waned in the rest of Europe. This statement may seem far from the truth, especially if we take into consideration the universal acclaim enjoyed by the eighteenth-century <u>philosophes</u> and the likes of Nietzsche in late nineteenth-century Europe.

But here we encounter for the first time what would become one of the most troubling phenomena of the modern age: the victory of appearance over substance, of propaganda over reality. In terms of creative thought, there can be little doubt that the genius of Descartes, Bacon, and Leibniz was superior by far to the cleverness of Voltaire and, with the probable exception of David Hume, to the eighteenth-century thinkers in general. Likewise, Nietzsche, Kierkegaard, Schopenhauer, and Marx hardly deserve to be compared to Kant. Yet in both eras the fame of these popular thinkers surpassed their originality. The most creative nineteenth-century thought came not from philosophy but from the sciences. Darwin and Freud illustrate the point.

In those cultures that were saturated with an established philosophical tradition the superficiality of the later Enlightenment and the inherent deficiencies of positivism, naturalism, neo-Kantianism, <u>Lebensphilosophie</u>, Lockian utilitarianism, and the new socialist doctrines could be easily accommodated. But it is interesting to note that in Spain where such academic buffers and supports did not exist to the same degree these same doctrines enjoyed scant success. Spain has long been the graveyard of overblown European doctrines.

On the other hand, it is also worth noting that certain

philosophers whose success was negligible in their own country were much more esteemed in Spain where the intellectual channels were not controlled by a rigid philosophic canon. Karl C. Friedrich Krause is a case in point. All but ignored in Germany, his thought became the basis of the "Krausist" school in Spain founded by Giner de los Ríos and his disciples. Wilhelm Dilthey is another example of a German thinker who was "discovered" in Spain thanks to Ortega and his school but who, aside from the respect Heidegger paid him, was hardly appreciated in Germany.

With the possible exception of Great Britain, Spain appears to be the country that most resolutely has refused to renounce its history, or more precisely, that variety of history which Unamuno called its "intrahistory." Yet we must add at once that this decision is more apparent in the forms of popular action and custom than in intellectual discourse. (I am persuaded that of all the countries with which I am somewhat acquainted, Spain is the one that least agrees with the images created by its intelligentsia. Of course, if this is a rule, there are splendid exceptions among its thinkers.)

For this reason, Spain has resisted with surprising tenacity the temptations of Jacobin revolution. Spain seems to have been too radical to be merely revolutionary. Not that the exacerbating problems usually identified by historians as revolutionary causes were missing in Spain. But we must not be duped by words and appearances: the fact that there have been several halting steps toward revolution—along with other kinds of disturbances and uprisings in recent centuries—shows convincingly that Spain lacks the revolutionary predisposition. (The anarchistic incidents in Catalonia and other parts of Spain seem to me to arise from other conditions that are beside or beyond, the points I am trying to make here.)

A marked difference between Spain and its offspring civilizations has been a surprising lack of similar immunity to revolutionary actions in Latin American countries. Occasionally we need to remind ourselves that if these countries resemble Spain in many ways, Spain barely resembles Latin America at all. In the matter of revolutionary tradition, for instance, bear in mind that unlike the United States with its inimitable—and unlikely—blend of Neoclassical liberalism, Protestant ethics, and British pragmatism, the countries of Latin America were formed in early nineteenth-century revolutionary and romantic molds that had only anemic manifestations in Spain. Generally speaking, this seems to be why nineteenth-century South America looked to France, not Spain, for cultural and political guidance. We could say that unlike Spain, they were genetically conditioned by revolution and were naturally more inclined to countries with a genuine revolutionary tradition, if we may use such a paradoxical expression. In one sense, the American republics are more "modern" than Spain, but it is not the usual sense and will require further commentary in due course.

The common assumption remains, however, that if revolution is a constant option in the Hispanic republics, it is because they inherited the trait from Spain and that what is so of the offspring must be true of the parent. For the mistaken view persists of Spain as a country wracked by wars and social violence. Naturally, Spain has experienced such misfortunes at certain moments of its history, but probably less so than most major nations. The difference lies in the curious tendency to presuppose that whereas violence in, say, France or England is the exception that confirms the general rule of stability, in Spain instability is taken to be the general rule and order, the exception.

Even more paradoxical is the fact that to the degree the modern age came to see itself as the heir of Jacobin revolution, Spain by definition appeared to be correspondingly "non-modern," which is only a semantic step from being labeled anti-modern.

No doubt this is one of the factors that gave rise to the so-called "Black Legend" that has stained the image of Spain in modern times. Not that students of Spanish history have been timid in pointing out the distortions and exaggerations of the "Legend," as the old work by Juderías and the more recent and better crafted book by Kamen make clear.[5] Yet until the creation of new historiographical methods by Menéndez Pidal, Ortega, and Marías, among others, and the historical reconstructions by Menéndez Pidal, Asín Palacios, Castro, Albornoz, and others, both the avid defenders and determined detractors of Spanish history began with the prior assumption that the Hispanic peoples of both hemispheres stood at an eccentric remove from the rest of the modern world.

C. SPANISH ORIGINS

The assumption of eccentricity as a constant of Spanish history led Ortega to seek its causal factors in ancient Iberian ethnicity. Let me summarize his arguments. He states in España invertebrada [Invertebrate Spain] (1921) that Spanish anomalies can be traced all the way back to the Visigothic era. He reasons that unlike the Franks and Saxons, kindred Germanic peoples who by their gift of leadership and organization shaped the collectivities that would become France and England, the Visigoths reached the Iberian peninsula already enervated by prolonged contact with decadent Roman civilization. As a consequence of this decreased vitality, the Goths were able to establish only an anemic aristocracy in Iberia. This, explains Ortega, was why they were so easily swept aside by the Islamic hordes in the eighth century and why also the feudal structure of medieval Iberia did not develop into the more complex forms characteristic of other European kingdoms. Furthermore, in later centuries this deficiency would create conditions unsuitable for the development of the select minorities that Ortega held were the fundamental component of the enduring cultures of other European countries, especially France, which he held up as the prototypical model nation. Spain did not experience the long elitist discipline that shaped other cultures. For this reason, he maintains in <u>Invertebrate Spain</u> that both the rapid rise of Spanish civilization at the beginning of the modern age as well as its early decline in the seventeenth century were the work of unguided and undisciplined popular forces. Throughout the vast Hispanic empire the only accomplishments were those things that its energetic but unorganized masses could do. Lacking true leadership they would become, and remain susceptible to, the manipulations of local <u>caudillos</u> and <u>caciques</u>.[6]

Stated in the bluntest way, therefore, Ortega claimed that Spain was decadent from birth, that it was afflicted with a genetic defect that rendered problematic sustained greatness. With due modifications, Ortega later presented a version of this view in <u>La rebelión de las masas</u> (1927) as he came to realize that his old paradigm of weakened or irresponsible minorities and undisciplined masses in Spain had become a generalized phenomenon of modern Europe.

In contrast to Ortega, Ángel Ganivet drew a different

conclusion from his meditations on Spanish culture. He argued that it is precisely the ignorant, unlettered masses who save nations, unlike the brilliant few whom he called <u>ladrones del alma colectiva</u> (thieves of the collective soul).[7] Seduced by bookish ideas that sap their faith in Goel and country, intellectuals are the first to falter under adversity. Furthermore, under the tutelage of these fickle elitists, the same human masses that were relativity happy as an anonymous collectivity become wretched as individuals.

This is yet another version of the phenomenon that Julien Benda called the <u>trahison des clercs</u> (the betrayal of the clerks) and Ortega described as the "desertion" of intellectuals.[8] This subversive irresponsibility on the part of modern intellectuals is an urgent theme that has yet to receive due consideration.

The theories of Américo Castro in <u>España en su historia</u> and <u>La realidad histórica de España</u> are cast in a very different mold, leaving aside from our consideration the inferior contentions of such writers as Eduardo Subirats, Juan Goytisolo or José Jiménez Lozano. Unlike Ortega, for whom the Arabic and Semitic element in Spain seemed to be of scant importance, Castro envisioned Spanish as a tripartite amalgam or mosaic of Moors, Jews, and Christians. In this he shares Ganivet's enthusiasm for the Semitic. It should be noted, however, that in Castro the bias is stronger, if not prejudicial, for he clearly favors the medieval Jewish and Moorish influences over the Christian, which he tends to dismiss as barbarous and ultimately repressive. It is interesting to note that even though they were poles apart in their conclusions, Castro and Ortega converge in odd agreement insofar as their tendency to disregard the indigenous Christian element of Spain is concerned. This suggests once again, though we shall not insist on it here, that possibly both thinkers were impacted by the pervasive inferiority complex that has troubled modern Spain.

Neither Ortega nor Castro seems to attribute much importance to the neo-Latin character of the Spanish language which allows almost direct access to Roman and Classical civilization as well as to other cultures derived from Latin, Catholic, and European sources. We can only imagine the cultural abyss that would have separated Spain from the West had the Arabic language permanently displaced Spanish. Because of Spain's Latin and Classical character, which persists as a transnational patrimony, the French, Portuguese, or Italian "foreigner" is much less "foreign" to the Spanish than a German or a Swede, to say nothing of non-Western people.

Castro's infatuation with the Semitic is so well known that no further commentary is needed here. We need not wonder that for the most part he ignores—as does Ortega—not only the civilizing force of Catholicism but also the main elements of what could be called the prior Iberian "infrastructure": well organized cities with their impressive cultural outreach, ecclesiastical law and hierarchy, aqueducts, roads, agriculture, and ranching. These components of Hispanic culture date from the Roman era and surpass in importance the later Semitic contributions that constitute additions to a preexisting civilization.

It is true that medieval Spanish populations often lived in barbarous circumstances and perhaps were inferior to their Romanized ancestors and disadvantaged in comparison to many of their Moorish and Jewish contemporaries. But this condition was hardly the fault of Catholic Christianity, as Castro and others imply, but the result of Islamic conquest and oppression.

We need to put to rest the myth that the Moors civilized Spain and spread learning to the whole of Europe. Despite undeniable Moslem contributions, it was not Islam that brought enduring enlightenment to Spain. Rather it was these same so-called "barbarous" Christians who saved the remnants of preexisting Latin and Classical civilization, including the neo-Latin language, Roman texts and Law, and the Christian faith from the cultural stagnation that eventually settled over the vast Islamic empire. We know now that the early splendors of Islam—medicine, architecture, learning—were not the products of its own ethos but borrowings from, or modifications of, the remnants of Classical civilization. In the long run these early advances vanished as a consequence of the Islamic failure to transcend its original fundamentalism. *If Islam were truly the prime civilizing element of Spain, then where, we must ask, are the splendid civilizations it should have fostered under similar conditions along the North African littoral where Islam displaced Christianity and Classical culture vanished for good?*

And can we not raise similar doubts about the supposedly superior organizing qualities of the Visigoths? According to Américo Castro, the Germanic invaders remained unassimilated and thus cannot be counted as Spanish at all, at least not until after the Moslem conquest. For Ortega, on the other hand, they were endowed with at least a modest fund of barbaric vitality that furnished what little feudal and elitist leadership Spain was to have throughout its history. But the truth is that this reputed "Germanic" vitality hardly coheres with the history of the Visigoths themselves. *For where during their extensive wanderings through many lands did the Goths build anything resembling an enduring civilization?* Can we not make the better argument that it was not what the Goths brought with them to

Spain but what they readily adopted once they got there—among other things, neo-Latin Spanish, the Catholic faith, and the remnants of Classical culture—that allowed them to transcend briefly their turbid and unstable history?

In either case, in the earlier decades of the twentieth century it became a habit to look beyond Spain itself to Islamic Africa or pagan Germany for major indices of Spanish character and history. This despite the fact that nothing remotely similar to Spain ever existed in either of these lands.

D. THE THEME OF 'SPANISH "DECADENCE"

It is a curious fact that unlike other Western nations, at least until recent times, Spain contended for centuries with questions of national decline and decadence. The fact that this perception substantially transcended real conditions and problems means, as I see it, that conventional attempts to explain it fall short. Later we shall examine certain alternatives.

As we have seen, Ortega argued that this decadence sprang from the diminished barbaric vigor of the primitive Visigoths, while for Américo Castro it was traceable to the error Spain committed by expelling the Jews and Moors. Let me add a parenthetical note to what I said earlier: although the Moors are credited for bringing civilization to Spain, they are also blamed for perceived Spanish backwardness. No doubt many of the same people who admire the Alhambra of Granada or the Great Mosque of Cordoba would also agree with the scornful comment attributed to Montesquieu: *L'Afrique commence aux Pyrénnées* (Africa begins at the Pyrennees).

In a general way, this ambivalent attitude toward Spain applies also to everything Spanish and Hispanic. On the one hand, there is a great deal of enthusiasm for this way of life. Think, for instance, of the popularity in the United States of Hispanic styles, music, art, food, literary and artistic themes, and not least the suggestive euphony of the Spanish language itself. (What would the American automobile industry do without a repertory of dramatic-sounding Spanish names for its cars and trucks, or how would hundreds of American cities find substitutes for romantic sounding Spanish names for their streets, subdivisions, malls, and markets, to say nothing of rivers, mountains, plains, and even States?

At the same time, however, there persists the forlorn image of the Hispanic world—constantly reinforced by the news media, missionaries, historians, sociologists, and "experts" in foreign policy—as part of the woeful "third world," a euphemistically destructive label pinned by the richer nations on those countries they have declared to be the world's misfits.

Thus, Hispanic societies both charm and repel foreign observers, for even though they are looked down on as politically untrustworthy and economically backward, they offer dazzling beauty and human attractiveness, as travel agencies everywhere attest. And who knows but what the travel agencies portray a truer image than many of the "experts."[9]

No doubt the most harmful effects of this general disqualification of the Hispanic world have been internal, in Spain of course but perhaps even more so in Hispanic America. The idea that to be Spanish or the cultural heir of Spain is the worst of all destinies has become a standard feature of ideological propaganda in Hispanic America and as such subject to sensationalist manipulations.

Probably this is why some countries, notably Mexico, extol

their aboriginal ancestry—the so-called *indigenismo* popularized in art and literature—and reject with matching antipathy reminders of their Spanish heritage. Probably for the same anti-Spanish reasons, other countries such as Argentina make much of their "Europeanism." Going a step further, the Cuban revolution not only rejects its Spanish past but also generally frowns on everything European and Western, favoring instead Cuba's African heritage and Marxist allegiance. All this—expressed in Spanish of course—tends to undermine the future possibilities of Hispanic countries, for more than the simple criticism of unfavorable situations and remediable problems, it amounts to a radical rejection of the Hispanic condition itself.

Believing themselves, therefore, to be the unlucky descendants of obscurantist and destructive Spain, the Hispanic peoples of both hemispheres are prone to a certain fatalism that often persuades them to see their sufferings and setbacks as evidence of their unhappy but unalterable destiny, when in reality they are simply the common, treatable problems experienced at one time or another by nearly all nations.

Despite essentially unchallenged assumptions about the causes of Spanish "decadence," in the scale of Spanish history itself the needle inclines toward the thesis of Julián Marías who points out in <u>España inteligible</u> that the famous expulsion of Jews and Moors actually preceded the two centuries of artistic and literary flowering we know as Spain's "Golden Age." Cervantes, Quevedo, Saavedra Fajardo, Tirso de Molina, Gracián, Zurbarán, Velázquez, Murillo, Lope de Vega, Moreto, and Calderón de la Barca are hardly names we can associate with decline. Rather they represent the pinnacle of Spanish genius precisely at the same time when supposedly Spain had entered into its decline.[10]

E. MODERN REVISIONISM

Modern Western historiography is rooted in eighteenth-century Enlightenment and as such still reflects much of the worldview of that era. It is a matter of considerable importance, for instance, that the basic nomenclature of modern history dates from that period. To this day we still think and speak of the "Dark Ages" (*âges ténébreux*), "Middle Ages," and the "Modem Age," terms that were—and still are—intellectually lax neologisms invented by Enlightenment writers such as Voltaire and Gibbon.

Naturally, in order for the so-called "Middle Ages" to exist there had to be a "before" and "after." For the eighteenth-century philosophes these flanking eras were the "enlightened" Classical Age of Greece and Rome and their own "modern" time. Like brilliant lights shining at both ends of a long dark time tunnel, they marked, respectively, the beginning and the end of the barbarous and benighted "middle" ages of Europe.

Heirs of the Enlightenment, we associate the Middle Ages with outlandish superstitions. A flat earth and the dread of sailing over its edge into the cosmic abyss, sea monsters, troglodytes, ogres, and other bizarre creatures have become the standard imagery of medieval European lore. But are these images an accurate picture of that time?

In his book Inventing the Flat Earth, Jeffrey B. Russell argues that many of these images were fabricated by modern thinkers—Gibbon, Voltaire, Diderot, and their intellectual contemporaries and descendants—whose aim was to ridicule and discredit the Middle Ages. Yet according to Russell, this slanderous portrayal of the Middle Ages did not become firmly fixed in the public mind—particularly in the English-speaking world—until the late nineteenth and early twentieth century as a result of polarizing debates over Darwinian evolution.

A surprising amount of evidence supports Russell's thesis, some of which he fails to include in his work. Consider, for instance, the notion of a flat earth.

Supposedly, modern scientists discovered the sphericity of the earth. Yet not only did the ancient Greeks—and probably the Egyptians—know that the earth was round but also calculated its circumference with reasonable accuracy. Later both Saint Augustine and Saint Thomas Aquinas spoke of a round earth, and in <u>Le Livre du Trésor</u> (The Book of the Treasure) (1265), an encyclopedic compilation of Classical and Medieval learning, Bruno Latini (or Brunet Latin in French) wrote that the Sun and the more distant planets were larger than the earth, while the Moon, Mercury, and Venus were smaller. Because the earth is round, he goes on to say, if there were nothing to block the way, a traveler could circle the world by setting out toward the west and returning from the east.[11] No doubt many ignorant people of the Middle Ages did believe the world was flat. For that matter, a surprising number of people still do. But not the educated class, and not experienced sailors like Columbus who observed the curvature of the earth every time they sailed from port.

Many of the same Enlightenment thinkers who strove to discredit the Middle Ages for reasons that we shall examine also looked askance at Spain and the Empire. The vehemence of these opinions seems disproportionate to the prevailing tranquility within the Hispanic world itself during the entire century. (Eighteenth-century Spain enjoyed the longest uninterrupted peace of any modern European nation. No major war occurred between 1715 and 1808.) By this time, Spain had long since assumed a secondary role in European diplomacy and hardly posed a military threat to other nations. Therefore, this Enlightenment animosity could hardly have been a reaction to Spain's modest international agenda in the eighteenth century. But then how does one explain it?

Julián Marías may have the answer. He suggests in <u>España inteligible</u> that in addition to old antipathies passed down from former times when Spain was at its zenith, this hostility was directed toward what Spain was, not what she was doing.[12] But this begs the question unless we provide certain clues to the ways in which Spain provoked the <u>philosophes</u>. Marías describes the first. Despite its reverses, eighteenth-century Spain, he points out, continued to be a formidable reality. Moreover, the Hispanic Empire (*las Españas*) was still essentially intact and functional, though on the defensive in Europe after the death of Philip II in 1598. We can add that even though Spain itself was minimally "present" in Europe during the first half of the century, the other imperial "Spains"—especially Mexico and Peru—continued to grow and consolidate. Christian and Catholic at its roots, the Empire constituted what the Enlightenment thinkers took to be an obscurantist barrier to their anticlerical ambitions.

But what Spain was and why its way of life aroused the ire of the Enlightenment intellectuals must be understood from yet another perspective. I stated earlier that many of the same thinkers who strove to discredit the Middle Ages and Christianity—Voltaire, Gibbon, Montesquieu, Condorcet, among others—also attempted to disqualify Spain. They summed up their vituperation in a label: "medieval." Spain, they claimed, had not experienced the Renaissance and, consequently, was incapable of participating in the Enlightenment. In short, it continued to be a medieval country: stagnant and monstrous.

What began as slander become, with time and repetition, an article of faith, and nowhere more so than in Spain itself which took the accusation very much to heart. Not until the Generations of 1898 would Spain begin to think of itself in other ways.

In an oblique way, the *philosophes* sensed a truth about Spain, but perhaps not the one they thought. It was not that Spain was simply "medieval" in the pejorative way they intended but rather that it represented a challenge and an alternative to European modernity that grew out of, and thus was not confined to, the Middle Ages. We could think of it as modernity's alter ego. As we shall see later, it stood uncertainly and unclearly for an altogether different species of modernity that could have been but except for fleeting moments and occasional hints was not. And Spain itself was at once the proponent and the victim of this frustrated alternative. For feeling itself called to champion another way of life, at the same time it was unable to avoid the triumphant example of nations fully committed to conventional modernity. Hence Spain's paralyzing ambivalence in modern times. Later we shall look at this topic from another perspective.

F *THE INQUISITION AND THE INDIES*

Of the several accusations of atrocities brought against Spain none surpasses in scope and gravity the so-called "Spanish Inquisition," particularly among Protestant nations. It has persisted over the ages as a grim metaphor of gratuitous cruelty, and Torquemada, the perverse human symbol of religious persecution.

Yet the Inquisition has its defenders, or at least its apologists. Menéndez y Pelayo, for instance, claimed that the Inquisition prevented the kind of religious wars that ravaged the Protestant countries, a claim that Arthur Kamen has supported in the work cited. Furthermore, Spain did not indulge in the famous "witch hunts" of Northern Europe, especially England and Germany, which took thousands of lives, dwarfing on a numerical scale the relatively few—most likely a few dozen, at most a few hundred—who died at the hands of the Inquisitors.

The "Spanish" Inquisition is of course misnamed. In truth it was a universal institution that tried its most celebrated cases, Galileo and Bruno, for instance, outside of Spain.[13] Furthermore, we have only to recall the martyrdom of Sir Thomas Moore and John Calvin's actions against Sebastian Castellio, Ami Perrin, Berthelier, Bolsee, and Michael Servetus to realize that religious persecution was generously distributed among Catholics and Protestants in that pious but vengeful age.

In modem times only the "destruction of the Indies" rivals the Inquisition in infamy. Today almost everything Father de las Casas had to say is taken as an article of faith. Thus, the Spanish are blamed for the disappearance of entire cultures along with their artifacts, libraries, art, and monuments. Eduardo Subirats claims as much in his strident book El continente vacío (The Empty Continent). There has been much intellectual anguish over the loss of archival records of civilizations perceived to be if not more advanced than Europe at least more humane. Supposedly all this was devastated by rapacious conquistadors whose lust for gold far outweighed their obedience to God.[14]

Sensational and accusatory, certainly, but is this what really happened in the Americas? To a certain degree, yes, we have only to read the accounts by Father Sahagún or Bernal Díaz del Castillo to erase any doubt that atrocities occurred during the Conquest.[15]

But a fair balance requires us to hear the rest of the story. In the first place, the Spanish were not the only ones guilty of atrocities in those wars. In the words of Andrés Bello, "Injustice, atrocities, and perfidy...have not been confined to the Spanish alone but apply to all races and to all times." [16] But the facts themselves argue more strongly than this bland excuse. When the Spanish reached Mexico in 1519 the number of people being sacrificed yearly in indigenous religious rituals surpassed by far the most exaggerated totals of all those who died at the hands of the Inquisition. The Spanish reacted with horror at these practices and as other explorers and missionaries have done with cannibalistic rites and human sacrifice in other parts of the world, quickly put an end to them.

These sixteenth-century Spanish explorers hardly had twenty-first century archeologists and scholars in mind as they proceeded with the conquest of the Americas, yet they are castigated for the oversight. In any case, if much was lost during the conquest, much was saved. Father Sahagún, for instance, spent years compiling—in the Nahuatl language—the chronicles and recording the cultural history of the indigenous peoples he served. Father Diego de Landa did much the same for the cultures of the Yucatan.

But there are more evident and visible factors to consider. The truth is that the overwhelming majority of the peoples, cities, and monuments of the native cultures did not perish, as Father las Casas, Lastarria, and others have claimed, but survive to this day in altered form. Far from being destroyed, they received the ingrafted Spanish or Portuguese cultures and were transformed into something else. To put it another way, America was created by this merger, though not without pain and trauma. One abiding proof of this process is that today the American countries preserve many things that remind one of Spain or Portugal, including things that have not survived in the mother countries, but they also contain many other things that have nothing to do with the European culture. Until recent years there was little in Spain (more in Portugal) that reminded one of the Americas. We could say, therefore, that this Iberian ingrafting radically transformed the future Americas, yet the strictly native dimensions of those cultures left few permanent traces in Iberia. This helps explain both the numerous affinities and substantial differences between Iberian and American cultures.

Despite popular use of the term, it is idle to speak of a "pre-Columbian America." Reality does not predate itself. America never existed before 1492 except in a purely telluric or geographical sense. But it would be equally incorrect to think of America simply as an Iberian transplant. More than a discovery, encounter, or conquest, the usual interpretative modes, America was an invention.

But to describe the Americas in these terms requires us to add some explanatory details. Unquestionably, both North and South America are relatively new historical realities, even though the exact nature of these realities has been the object of contradictory interpretations. Both are associated with unappealing features: the North with technological capitalism and puritanical narrowmindedness and the South with impractical social idealism and a strong tendency to corruption and absolutism. From this angle, the United States appears crass and altruistic, while Latin America seems perpetually tentative. In <u>Ariel</u> (1900) José Enrique Rodó saw these differences as a contrast between the materialism of the North and the idealism of the South, with the moral needle pointing to the Hispanic cultures.

In both cases, we seem to encounter a unique form of realism which, for all its defects, radiates from the future from which it receives periodic infusions of hope and idealism. Perhaps this explains the seemingly provisional character of American reality, especially in English-speaking America, where we often have the impression—and the experience to reinforce it—that on any given day the impermanent reality before us may vanish and be replaced by something else. Our general impression is that American reality is thoroughly permeated by the unreal.

Unlike the first English colonists who desired above all unpopulated lands, and who therefore watched with a certain satisfaction as smallpox and other epidemics devastated the native inhabitants of North America—in Massachusetts, for example—the Spanish sought settled populations and established cities for the dual purpose of adding yet other "Spains" to the Empire and converting more souls to the Christian faith. Like nearly every other conquering army in history, they were not immune to personal gain and plunder. There was pillage and serious abuse, but it is important to point out that these outrages were recognized as such and were never standards of behavior condoned by the Monarchy and the Church.

The decrees issuing from both institutions were surprisingly idealistic and enlightened for that time. In fact, they may have been too idealistic and thus unenforceable. To point to one example, unlike the English-speaking world where doubts about the full humanity of dark races lingered well into the seventeenth century (and in the North American South until the nineteenth), sixteenth-century Spain and Portugal acknowledged not only the rights of native populations to equal protection before the law but also to their human equality and susceptibility to salvation.

Despite sensationalist images of a Spain surfeited with gold stolen from enslaved native peoples, the truth remains that America cost Spain more than it rendered. Andrés Bello notes that the Americas were for Spain "...a cause of depopulation and backwardness."

Once the Empire was formed, Spain itself was but one of the several "Spains." The riches of America flowed to the imperial crown and thence to their European creditors, not to Spain itself, which like the other dominions was subject to the Hapsburgs. On the other hand, the population of Spain declined drastically due mainly to emigration to the New World, by some accounts as much as forty percent between 1550 and 1700, falling from an estimated ten million to six million. Not until the end of the eighteenth century would the Spanish population again surpass ten million. By the end of the seventeenth century whole areas of Spain were left desolate without populations to cultivate the land. This decline, occurring at a time when the populations of neighboring nations were rapidly increasing, has to be taken as a prime factor in Spain's so-called "decadence."

Unlike the English for whom the colonies were either a business or a religious haven and whose priorities were the displacement or extermination of native peoples, the Spanish and Portuguese assumed the transcendental task of "civilizing peoples and giving expansion to ideas." These are Ángel Ganivet's words, and he goes on to say: "Let us leave it to other peoples to practice their utilitarian colonization and let us continue our traditional system which, for better or worse, is ours after all."

G. THE SPANISH "COLONIAL" SYSTEM

I have given a misleading title to this section, but it serves to call attention to the historical misunderstanding of what Ganivet referred to as Spain's "traditional system." For even though the Spanish Empire preceded by nearly a century the British, Dutch, and French system of "colonies," these became the measure by which the overseas viceroyalties would be interpreted and understood. Whereas British, Dutch and French colonies were dependencies of the mother country or its commercial subsidiaries and strictly subject to them, the Spanish realms were essentially self-governing, autonomous viceroyalties and in any case answerable not to Castile nor even to united Spain but to the Emperor. **Spain itself did not possess these kingdoms but was itself one of the several "Spains" within the Empire.**

Naturally, however, its relationship with the "other" Spains was not one of simple parity, for it furnished the settlers and missionaries that gave them their Hispanic character in the first place. But these "American" Spaniards believed themselves to be no less Spanish than their Iberian counterparts. This is why in seventeenth-century Cuba economist Francisco de Arando y Parreno could refer to himself as an "overseas Spaniard." Only in the nineteenth-century in imitation of the great colonial powers of Europe—particularly France with which Spain was dynastically allied through the so-called "Family Pact" of the Bourbons—did the Spanish begin to think of Cuba, Puerto Rico, and the Philippine Islands as colonies and to treat them accordingly. With predictably ill results, it should be added.

But these remaining colonies or possessions were never on a level with the former "Spains" of Peru and Mexico. Until the end of the eighteenth-century, for example, Cuba, the most important of these peripheral territories, had little population and insufficient resources to maintain itself. Official expenses were covered by a _situado,_ or monetary supplement sent from Mexico City. The abortive British invasion of 1762 alerted Spanish officials to the strategic importance of the island, and around 1790 the administration of Captain General Don Luis de las Casas began working in earnest toward its economic development.

During the first half of the nineteenth century under commercial pressure from the British and the threat of French revolutionary ideals and annexation by the United States, Cuban governors opted for a policy of despotic persecution. Thus José Antonio Saco was exiled in 1834 and the poet Plácido was executed by firing squad. Though officially banned by Spain, a clandestine slave trade continued which Cirilo Villaverde described with considerable insight and sensitivity in his novel Cecilia Valdés.

Probably these imitative "colonial" policies introduced in the nineteenth century explain why in comparison to the wave of anguish produced in Spain in 1898 by the loss of the remnants of the old empire, the first "reduction" of 1824, which was much more definitive, occurred with relatively little commentary or soul searching by the Spanish populace.

In 1824 the Spanish still believed that rather than possessions or colonies of Spain, the Indies were, as they always had been, dominions of the monarchy, which at the time was regarded with considerable popular repugnance because of the despotism of Fernando VII and the reactionary support of France ("The hundred thousand sons of Saint Louis"). Because Spain and the Spanish did not possess the Americas in the first place, they could hardly lose them.

By 1898 the Spanish had taken a very different posture regarding what it now considered to be its "colonies." And this change of perspective allows us to surmise that during the course of the nineteenth century Spain underwent a process of "Europeanization" with the adoption of this and other political, literary, scientific, and philosophical ideas. Consider the tentative inroads made by imported doctrines: Krausism, literary naturalism, Comtian positivism, Nietzschean thought, as well as the older forms of rationalism. One could argue in this context that the polemic raised by members of the so-called "Generation of 1898" and their immediate predecessors over the proposed "Europeanization" of Spain was somewhat after the fact. It was perceived to be a genuine option only because it was already a reality.

It is interesting to speculate that under a conventional "colonial" format in, say, the British or Dutch style probably Spain would have been unable to govern the full Empire of the Indies. Its immense size and logistical demands—standing armies spread over vast territories, governmental and civil complexities, and the need for countless technical and bureaucratic personnel—would have taxed Spain's modest resources far beyond her limit. On the other hand, the "Empire" between 1824 and 1898 was reduced to sufficiently modest dimensions to give Spain at least the illusion of being a colonial power in the European mold.

As for the uprisings that eventually ended the neo-colonial structure, there is one factor that perhaps has been overlooked: the massive immigration to Cuba and Puerto Rico of "Europeanized" Spaniards, especially during the second half of the nineteenth century. This sounds paradoxical until we realize that these new arrivals—mostly Galicians and Catalonians, to judge by the lists of passengers disembarking in Havana, Santiago, San Juan, and other ports—were imbued with the European understanding of colonies as well as the volatile revolutionary ideals of equality and independence. Most of these immigrants soon became "Americanized" and identified with their new country, although some would return to Spain as the well-known *indianos* of nineteenth-century Spanish novels. As Spaniards they resented colonial policies that tended to make them subservient to the mother country, and as Cubans or Puerto Ricans, they could no longer comfortably call themselves "overseas Spaniards." Paradoxically, this secondary "hispanization" of Cuba and Puerto Rico became a catalyst in the struggle for freedom from Spain. The case of José Martí, the "Apostle" of Cuban independence, is revealing. Of Catalonian ancestry, his family had recent ties to the mother country.

Of course, the links to Spain, acknowledged or not, are very strong in all Spanish-speaking countries. But it would be interesting to identify the historical period to which these bonds correspond. Some countries—Mexico, Colombia, Chile, and Peru—have collective memories of the Spain of the sixteenth and seventeenth centuries and have received only sporadic influences since. Chilean writer José Victoriano Lastarria wrote in 1842, for example, that "...the Spain of today is the Spain of the sixteenth century." To this day they preserve a quaint and half-legendary image of the Spain of the Conquest and the viceroyalties.

On the other hand, Cuba and Puerto Rico mostly remember nineteenth-century "colonial" Spain with its middle class, commercial traits. Perhaps this is why in comparison to the countries associated with Golden Age Spain there is a noticeable lowering of the Catholic temperature and a correspondingly greater entrepreneurial aptitude in the islands.

The case of Father Hidalgo in Mexico is quite different. Also the son of Spaniards, Hidalgo uttered his famous grito (cry) of independence in 1810 not with the revolutionary intention of abolishing the social and religious structure of Mexico but with the aim of preserving it. Following the French invasion of Spain in 1808 and the apparent triumph of revolutionary and Napoleonic ideals on the European continent, Hidalgo acted to prevent the infiltration of what he perceived to be anti-Catholic ideas emanating from radicalized France but filtered through subjugated and gallicized Spain.

Almost simultaneously with Father Hidalgo's revolt in Mexico, there occurred a movement toward conciliation in the Constitutional Congress of Cadiz in 1812. There, representatives from all over the Empire produced a document that for a brief historical moment combined many ancient Hispanic values with the most intelligent ideas of the Enlightenment. It was to become the basis of all subsequent Spanish constitutions. Not only was it imbued with respect for men and women alike—and not merely the abstract "rights of man"—but also with the moderating influence of thinkers like Father Feijóo and Jovellanos who advocated, among other things, respect for the Church and the Christian faith. In the best sense of the word, the Constitution of 1812 was a "romantic" document, but in the moderate Spanish mold, as Julián Marías has shown.[17] We can only speculate on what the history of Spain—and Hispanic America—would have been had not the enlightened provisions of the Cadiz Constitution been overshadowed in the nineteenth century by the rise of divisive political parties and rancorous partisanship.

H. ERRORS OF INTERPRETATION

It is apparent in view of what we examined that at least two fundamental errors have customarily hindered a full understanding of Spanish and Hispanic history. The first consists of an old tendency to think of Spain as an isolated reality and to ignore its historical and geographical context. In other words, Spain is treated as though it were alone in the world. Ortega described this isolation as the "Tibetanization" of Spain and warned his fellow Spaniards not to forget that Spain is also situated in Europe.

The objection may be raised that this contrastive and isolationist method has been the historiographical norm in attempting to decipher the nature and history of Spain. Yet tacit references to this Western and European context are unavoidable, for Spain can only be regarded as anomalous in a context of so-called "normal" and thus normative societies and countries. It has to be compared to something normal in order to be adjudged abnormal.

This insistence on Spanish "eccentricities" tends to convert Spain (or Europe seen from the opposing viewpoint) formally into the alien "other." Two extremist options thus seem to beckon: either Spain is the anomalous and eccentric country of popular history or Europe itself appears as the intrusive, oppressive alternative aggressively pressing in on the Spanish way of life.

The second error arises as a radicalization of the first. It consists of converting Spain's supposed "abnormality" itself into the norm of Spanish history and of extracting from this condition certain fateful consequences: lack of historical coherence, deficiencies of the national Spanish and Hispanic character, political ineptitude, and so on. In other words, if abnormality itself is seen as "normal," then it follows that abnormal behavior becomes the natural behavior one would expect from Hispanic peoples. It is a tortured logic that for centuries has distorted Hispanic history, and what is worse, Hispanic life.

In the light of these exegetical deficiencies the better procedure is to explain Spanish reality from within Spain itself, as we saw earlier. But here we must add a caution against the sort of exclusivity that has distorted earlier interpretations. To say that we must understand Spain from within and on its own terms also means that we must take its real circumstances into account, the main ingredient of which is Europe (or more accurately in our day, the West). Earlier I spoke of the "Europeanization" of Spain that occurred in the nineteenth century and led to the debates on the topic by the generations of 1898. But this clarification is misleading unless we recall Ortega's assertion that Europe has always been the constitutive nucleus of Spanish culture.

This means that a serious analysis of Spanish history must account for the shaping weight and force of Europe. Probably many of the so-called "anomalies" of Spanish history will be found to consist of hidden but real pressures originating outside of Spain. Consider, for example, the recent effects on Spain of certain international doctrines and ideologies. Socialism, Marxism, fascism, and the prevailing forms of Western democracy are examples we could point out.

But this prior "Europeanization" must be understood in the same phenomenological way it has functioned. If it is true that Europe is the informing reality of Spain and other nations, it is also true that it has never functioned as a monolithic cultural bloc. Historically speaking, Europe has exercised its exemplary leadership only through the diversity of its nations. Competition, not compliance, has been the supreme expression of Europeanism. In modern times countries have competed for European leadership and have resisted as forms of lese-Europeanism—Prussia, Napoleon, Hitler, the Soviet Union—all tyrannical attempts to force them into a single mold.

I. AL-ANDALUS AND SPAIN

In the broadest sense, the circumstances of a country, like those of a person, are necessarily universal. By definition, they consist of all surrounding physical and historical reality, including, among others, cultural and demographic factors. Spanish circumstances naturally include Islamic reality in its multiple forms: at certain moments of its history as a menacing force, at others, as a defeated power belonging to the past. We have seen a gamut of opinions concerning the importance of Islam in Spain. For Américo Castro, Ganivet, and others, the Semitic presence, including the Jewish people of course, is definitive. On the other hand, for other thinkers—Menéndez y Pelayo, Julián Marías, García Morente, among others—Christianity is the paramount influence. Perhaps it is possible to blend the two premises, provided we go beyond them and assume a new perspective.

The history of a country, like the biography of a person, comes to light and acquires its full meaning only in a context of real options. Who we strive to be becomes clear only when we also know who we could have been, and equally important, who we would not or could not be. The selected life—for life is selection—shines in the afterglow of other lives we have foregone. Human history consists not of simple data or chronicles but instead includes—or at least, alludes to—the ideal panorama of what could have been, but was not. The most fundamental epistemology is simply this: to understand life, or anything else for that matter, is to understand why some things happen and others do not. Historical understanding always transcends fact and becomes what its name implies: a story.

If we omit the narrative structure of history, all the elements of Spanish history—Christians, Jews, Moslems, Romans, Visigoths, prehistoric peoples can lay essentially the same claim to historical importance. The result is an interesting mosaic but inert like all mosaics and the very contrary of history, which is always a story in progress.

But to insist on the "story" in which history consists, is not to assume that all national narratives are equally compelling and significant. Some nations, like some people, have only a minimal story to tell, and only an overblown egalitarian spirit would cause us to think otherwise. Lacking the necessary creative will and discipline, or perhaps thwarted by historical circumstances beyond their control, they seldom rise above mundane life and immemorial routine. In any case, this human and historical limitation is not primarily a function of natural resources or the lack thereof, as we customarily think. Generally speaking, never have these been more abundant, especially if we include the artificial resources created by art and technology. Profound differences separate the two classes: natural resources help us to live in world of the possible, while art and technology allow us to subdue the impossible.

Despite their differences, both natural and artificial "resources" can be defined as such only when they function as appropriated components in our plans and projects, in the largest sense, the "biographical" narrative of a nation. To put it another way, unless there is a prior human design for the world there are no resources as we understand the term. For it is not resources that make man, but man who makes his resources. [18]

Within a larger template, history supports the point I have been making. Perhaps it is no accident that many of the civilizations that have made the deepest imprint on the destinies of the West—Israel, Greece, Rome, England, Spain—were poorly or modestly endowed with natural resources. Their greatness lay not in natural resources but in the inimitable way they understood and organized human life. They achieved a biographical richness despite the natural limitations of their respective worlds.

A few years ago, it became politically unpopular to attribute superior or absolute originality to certain countries, particularly those of Christian and Western origin. Today there exists the curious notion, probably deriving from anti-colonial sentiments, that all territories enjoy equal dignity as countries. This makes for a neatly colored map and a full roster at the United Nations, but it also creates unstable conglomerations that are countries in name only.

In the case of Spain there was no question of its historical Christian vision by which it identified itself and which we understand in apposition to Islamic Al-Andalus. For that matter, we can formally declare that while Al-Andalus was located **in** the territory we call Spain, it was never within **cultural** Spain. We must not be deluded by geographical proximity, since this manner of being present does not mean it was also a part of Spain, except in a derived and misleading sense. Rather, despite its geographical proximity, Spain's relationship to Al-Andalus was one of rejection because of its alien nature and its non-Spanish "narrative," in a word, because of its unassimilable "otherness."

The point I wish to make here is that we must distinguish between Spain and Al-Andalus not to diminish the latter's importance but so as to give it proper consideration from another perspective. The enormous reality of Islam, of which Iberian Al-Andalus was but the most visible fragment, radically pressured and conditioned Spain for centuries. **Therefore, although Al-Andalus did not figure in the Christian and European "narrative" on which Spain was structured, it drastically configured it, as the gravity of a planet affects the orbit of another nearby.** Thus, it would be impossible to understand the nature and narrative of Spain without taking its Islamic "configuration" into account, but in no way can Spain be "reduced" to Islam, as a mosaic might be reduced to its component pieces.

Far from being an inorganic and haphazard multicultural amalgam, Spain can best be thought of as a drama in which the succeeding acts and scenes are understandable in the light of those that precede and follow them. But even this description is incomplete if we fail to take into account the dramatic force that creates these scenes in the first place. That force was the will to be Christian against all odds. In fact, Spanish Christianity contains at its core this adversarial sense.

But there was a second force at work. We have been acknowledging all along with Ortega that from the beginning Spain has also been in Europe as part of another drama, and by doing so we have insinuated naturally that Europe is also in Spain. This leads to a premise already introduced but which from now on we will insist on more forcefully: Spanish history comes to light only within a European context, and the corollary is no less true that certain dimensions of European history—the Renaissance, for instance—become clear by taking into account the hitherto largely ignored history of Spain.

From this viewpoint we see that far from being an exclusively Spanish or Iberian phenomenon, Islam pressured European civilization for many centuries. To begin with, it defined the very geography of Europe. Julián Marías explains in <u>España inteligible</u> that the boundary established along the old <u>Mare Nostrum</u> by the Islamic conquests did not mean simply the loss and disappearance of the southern half of Christendom and the Classical world. Instead. these Islamic kingdoms remained as a menacing and inaccessible presence. Other Europeans may forget that for a thousand years and well into the nineteenth century the plight of Christian captives in Islamic Turkey and Africa was a theme of European literatures just as Moslem piracy was a grievous political concern. Furthermore, the planned retaking of the original Christian lands of the Middle East and Africa, often tried and as often foiled, remained the supreme objective of Medieval Europe.[19]

In early modern times with the waning of the Islamic threat and the uncontested hegemony of Europe and the West, other Europeans began to forget their millennial confrontation with Islam. Beginning in the eighteenth-century the Enlightenment writers and physiocrats, who were determined to free themselves from their historical past, carne to believe that the old struggles between Spain and Islam had nothing to do with Europe. Precisely because of Spain's long involvement with the Islamic world, the philosophes thought of it as being something less than European, conveniently but inappropriately forgetting how radically Islam had shaped their own history.

The Spanish had a better memory. The celebrated Spanish "abnormality," which to some extent consists of preserving both its determination to be Christian and the memory of the Islamic presence, thus turns out to be a greater faithfulness to historical reality. Here we find the very essence of Spain: the irrevocable determination to be Christian and European against great odds that it could realistically hope to be so. For centuries <u>Al-Andalus</u>, Eastern, Islamic, and the antithesis of everything European, threatened a cornered Spain, which was much less a factual reality than its ancient adversary. Modernity tends to relegate Spain to the rear guard of the European march, but for hundreds of years and from a different perspective it served as the shock troop and vanguard in the seemingly interminable European struggles with Islam.

It is true there were lapses in this strange Spanish will to be what seemingly Spain could not hope to be, and this explains in part the periods of coexistence, the satrapies, alliances, and other interludes in the so-called Middle Ages. Despite these pauses, however, the Spanish never lost their determination to be Christian and European. But this decision was not a simple matter of "being" Spain in the presence of <u>Al-Andalus.</u> Spain never settled for tolerant coexistence, even though for long centuries it was forced by circumstances to endure Islam. From the beginning it strove to reconstruct something materially lost but ideally preserved. **For this reason, it was not a matter of a conquest or annexation of Moslem lands but a "reconquest" of what the enemy had seized but which the Spanish had never surrendered.** In this unyielding resolve lies the principal difference between the Christians of North Africa and those of Iberia. The African Christians bowed to their fate and soon vanished from history, while the Spanish rejected their apparent Islamic destiny and survived to create a unique civilization.

The guiding ideal of Spanish Christians was to restore "lost Spain" which had existed, if at all, ever so briefly in Visigothic times. But the more tenuous the reality, the purer the ideal from which sprang the Spanish fervor and sense of prior claim over Iberia during the Reconquest. Nothing could be farther from the notion of a cultural "mosaic." Spain had been Christian before and by the grace of God and force of arms it would be Christian once again. Hernando de Acuña said it best in these exuberant verses:

One faith and one shepherd in the land One monarch, one empire, and one sword.

Time and again in their history the Spanish have responded to the call to rescue a traumatized and errant Spain either defeated by foreign invaders or brought to its knees by its own ineptitude and internal decadence. Seldom has this urgent quest been fully successful, and often the Spanish themselves have abandoned the consuming task. Yet over the ages it has remained an irrevocable moral imperative that has taken various forms: by means of arms in an earlier age, through science, letters, and thought in more recent times. But in all the immense commotions that have shaken the Spanish spirit we find a continuity in a passionate, questing faith, supremely sure and unwavering in earlier ages, in later centuries beset by rationalistic doubts, yet at all times profound and moving. Spain was born as the improbable ideal of being what she could not reasonably expect to be. And herein lies a baffling paradox of the Spanish character. I repeat that the Spanish have always respected reality above all else, but now I must add that they have never felt enslaved by it.

For from the beginning the realistic Spanish spirit has also exhibited a quixotic idealism which we may define—but not limit—as the refusal to yield before the impossibilities of destiny. If earthy Sancho Panza governs the prosaic Baratarias of Spanish life, Don Quixote rises to lead the quest for its ideal Dulcineas.

As we have seen, even though it has always been a matter of restoring "lost Spain," the task has taken different forms over the centuries. Thus. the restorative fervor which in earlier times took the form of territorial conquests under the exemplary leadership of Castile, in more recent centuries has manifested itself as successive intensifications of the Spanish way of being, that is, as new spiritual conquests. In this regard, nothing was more typical than the labors performed by the Generation of 1898 (as I prefer, "generations") whose "lyric recastilianization" of Spain stands as a new and permanent enrichment of the Spanish mode of being.

Finally, I have been insisting all along that Spain cannot be understood apart from Europe. But exactly what does this mean? We began this chapter by repeating Ortega's question, what is Spain? We conclude it by asking another: what is Europe? The answer to these and associated questions is our next task.

Chapter 3:
Spain and Europe

A. INVENTING THE FUTURE

What is Spain? This omnibus question, the leitmotif of the thinkers of 1898, implies another always presupposed and thus seldom stated: what is Europe? While not an immediate answer to either query, these metaphorical words of Ortega serve as our point of departure for responding to both. Europe, he remarks, is that "...swarm of Western peoples who from the ruins of the ancient world began their flight through history...."[1] As a conglomeration of culturally kindred peoples, Europe was launched into history from its fragmented heritage of Classical Mediterranean civilization.

This unique projective nature has conditioned European life in radical ways that we shall examine in the pages ahead. And if we accept the premise that Spain is in Europe and formed from the same historical substance as its neighbors, then it stands to reason that these characteristic European traits will also resonate in the matrix of Spanish civilization. And if this is true, then it follows that in order to understand Spain we must attempt to trace the general European parameters of its circumstance and history.[2]

Because the European condition is by nature projective and unfinished, we cannot restrict it to the past. The many-sided legacy of the Classical world functions not only as the primary historical component of European civilization but also as an ever present and recurrent ideal that has acted for centuries as the transcendent destiny of European peoples. Europe was their starting point and also their destination, and this imparts to European life not only a common historical unity but also a marked futuristic inclination.

On the other hand, history is replete with civilizations—in truth, almost all—that have lived transfixed in their immemorial past, sordid or splendid as the case may be.[3] **Very few, and none so much as the Europeans, have lived from the future.** More importantly, we discover that far from being simply the troubling enigma it represents for other cultures, to Europeans the future appears malleable and promising. It emerges as pure potentiality. This is why historically they have tended to regard the future not so much as what will be as what can be. If throughout most of human history the majority of cultures have viewed the future as the unfolding of predetermined fate, Europeans have looked on it as a function of human life friendly to their aspirations and forgiving of their errors. Other peoples endured the future but only Europeans believed they could create it. And this novel conviction set European civilization on a historical course marked by a degree of creativity, and innovation unparalleled in the history of the world.

There are, or have been, then, many peoples of a fatalistic bent whose future is limited to what will be. And the world accordingly obliges them. In one sense they have no future but merely repeat yesterday and today.

Let us exaggerate to make the point: **the future is Europe's greatest invention**. This is why also European peoples "incline" more or less enthusiastically to the future, incorporating it into their life and counting on it for fulfillment. Instead of being the horizon of uncertainty or mere dread, it becomes the arena of possible happiness. Rather than the graveyard of life, it becomes the wellspring of hope.

Naturally the future also includes eventual personal death and the apparent end of our earthly aspirations. All the rivers of life run into the sea of death, says Jorge Manrique, and in this mortal passing a universal egalitarianism vividly dramatized in the Medieval Dances of Death, obliterates the ranks of the mighty and reveals the final vanity of all worldly claims to honor and distinction. For believers, there remains the further hope of a paradise beyond this life, yet the next world, though attainable, exists at a contrapuntal remove from this earthly existence.

Where, then, is the virtue of this life and where the justification of hope in the future? The general human responses over the ages have tended to be pessimistic variations the single theme of mortal inevitability. The fatalist, the hedonist, the stoic, the existentialist, and, not least, many religious followings all share the premise that Cicero called the *confatalia*, or common fate of mankind, and differ only in their secondary reactions to mankind's short and brutal destiny in this world. James Shirley's lament is typical of many writers across the ages:

> *The glories of our blood and state*
> *Are shadows, not substantial things;*
> *There is no armour against fate...*
> ("Contention of Ajax and Ulysses III")

But the repetition of this error does not make it true. Even though recent European thinkers tire us with such sinister clichés about death, the creative idealism that historically has distinguished European civilization reveals very different attitudes toward mortality. I said earlier that in the *Coplas* of

Spanish poet Jorge Manrique Death acts as the great leveler of men and the ravager of love and life. But the <u>ubi sunt</u> theme of a bygone time with its colors, loves, beauties, and delights is not the whole story of that sublime work. For the exemplary life of the poet's father, Grand Master Don Rodrigo, does not simply vanish, nor do his heroic deeds disappear with him. His valor persists, his example lingers, his courage abides, perhaps forever. Greatness comes from doing. As Don Quixote tells Sancho, "No one is more than anyone else unless he does more."

Only in an abstract sense does Death appear to annihilate and level all people. When we have known them as persons, as Jorge Manrique knew his father, death consecrates at once the irreplaceable character of their life and deeds. In a double sense this high striving is worthy to be emulated. For on the one hand, it leaves a heroic measure for generations yet unborn in this world, and on the other, honor and fame accompany the departed into the next and there count also in the eternal reward:

And since, O noble and undaunted,
Your hands the paynim's blood have shed
In war and tourney, —
Make ready now to take the vaunted
High guerdon you have merited
*For this great Journey!*4

It has often been said that late medieval people like Jorge Manrique lived in an age of faith, but if true this statement is also incomplete. For it was not merely a matter of looking to the next world and overlooking this one but also of believing that this life had its own meaning and value, even though its claims were necessarily of lesser magnitude. As Gómez de la Serna once remarked, medieval people could be "proud of their soul," and this pride—always susceptible to misunderstanding and exaggeration—quite apart from their station in life gave them a sense of self-worth that our age would be hard pressed to match or understand. Modern man is more apt to depend on his civil status rather than on his spiritual reality. For with the evaporation of faith, modern man naturally lost his soul—or at least thought he had—and with it his ultimate self-assurance, becoming, in the words of Sartre, "a useless passion."

But try as he might—and he has—Western man finds no real happiness in merely enjoying the interval between birth and death, as philosopher George Santayana put it. For Santayana's formula implies an existence not only devoid of final significance but also lacking the dynamic and hopeful movement toward the future that has always characterized Western life. No wonder Western people instinctively repudiate such a circumscribed life.

To believe in a malleable tomorrow, to live with one foot already in the future, as it were, is to be ethically and pragmatically obliged to take responsibility for it. Hence the probing curiosity and characteristic alertness of the Western mind, traits that differ so markedly from the incurious routine and human stasis evident in almost all other traditional cultures.

In most non-European cultures, and I have in mind those that have not been overwhelmed by European and Western contact, intelligence seems to have consisted traditionally in the wisdom to seek and follow ancient life pathways. High and noble conformity to immemorial beliefs is thus the supreme human virtue in the non—European world, and genius could be defined as the ability to repeat in an exemplary manner the hallowed models of the past. Probably this more or less universal expectation is why the sages and shamans of nearly all other cultures bear such a resemblance to one another.

On the other hand, European intelligence is cast in an altogether different mold. Not content with conformity, it readily rejects the old in search of the better. Ultimately nothing is too sacred to question, nothing too divine to probe. Hence the European predisposition to sacrilegious thought and revolutionary upheaval. This is why other cultures often fear the European way of thinking as a scandal and an affront. In the best of times European thought has been an enlightened model to imitate, at the worst, a heretical abomination to oppose. If the non-European sees virtuous conformity to unquestioned tradition as the supreme good, the European senses in it an eventual betrayal of his very condition.

In moments of high confidence in its visionary control of the future—the era we call the Renaissance, the Enlightenment, much of the nineteenth century—the European mind is remarkable—if not always admirable—in its innovative daring and creative élan. But when it loses heart and confidence, as it has progressively since the eighteenth century, then philosophical nihilism clouds its vision of life and poisons the world around it. In the modern age wave after wave of enlightenment has swept out of Europe to seduce and conquer the world, and with almost the same imperialistic regularity its dire doctrines about humanity's helpless condition have infected the earth with spiritual dry rot. Bertrand Russell's words are typical of this gloomy vein: "Brief and powerless is Man's life; on him and all his race the slow, sure doom falls pitiless and dark. Blind to good and evil, reckless of destruction, omnipotent matter rolls on its relentless way..."[5]

B. THE DUALITY OF SPANISH FUTURISM.

Within this general futuristic paradigm Spain deserves special attention, but perhaps not in its customary modern role as the "sick man of Europe." We have seen that like other European cultures Spain arose from the remnants of the Christianized and Classical world and in this regard shares a fundamental "Europeanism" with its neighbors. And we have also seen how Islamic, Visigothic, and other influences helped to shape and configure Spanish culture at the margins without noticeably affecting its core.

The Spanish language itself neatly illustrates these distinct levels of influence. There is next to nothing Arabic or Germanic in the morphology and structural syntax of the Spanish language, even though both languages, and particularly Arabic, contributed many isolated words and expressions to its vocabulary.

All this seems clear enough, but these similarities to other European societies do not tell the whole story. For at the dawn of the modern age in Spain we also find an interesting redoubling of the generalized European tropism toward the future. On the one hand, Spaniards preserved the collective memory of Classical times and like their neighbors shared the ideal of a restored European and Christian unity. When Emperor Charles V proposed to other European rulers the Spanish vision of a pan-Christian Europe, what has been called <u>Universitas Christiana</u>, which was to consist of a coalition of Christian princes, he was responding to this thousand-year-old European vision. Historian Manuel Fernández Álvarez hints of this intensity: "In the mandate of Charles V there is a lesson of the ethical sense of the ruler, which is what differentiates him from the other sovereigns of Europe."[6]

But there is another factor in Spain that is much less apparent in other European countries. If other Europeans kept alive the memory of ancient Classical unity and moved haltingly toward its eventual restoration, the Spanish also responded, and indeed more immediately and aggressively, to the ideal of "lost Spain." Whether or not Visigothic <u>Hispania</u> was the first iteration of Spain is really a moot question. If not a full-fledged historical reality, at least the ideal of a unified Spain served to motivate Spaniards to make it so. Perhaps they sought for what never existed in the full sense, but the very imperfections of Spanish reality urged them on toward its completion:

They sought for things that never were,
and yet must ever be.

In any case, for Spaniards the first step in restoring the lost unity of ancient Christian and Classical civilization in which all European cultures were rooted was to wrest Spain away from Islam. In this sense we can say that the Reconquest was an eminently "European" undertaking, even though few Europeans carne to the aid of Spain in its war against Islam.

This dual pursuit of both destinies—lost Spain and the lost unity of the Classical age—gave Spain a historical complexity and a relatively higher Christian temperature that have not yet been fully decoded and assimilated. (Perhaps it is no accident that of all the major European languages Spanish is the only one with a term—*ilusión*—which adequately expresses the futuristic concept of enthusiasm we have been discussing.) Accelerated by its dual ideals, it should come as no surprise that Spain moved sooner than neighboring kingdoms into the basic configuration of a modern state. To cite but a single "modern" feature, unlike the medieval armies of previous centuries which consisted of seasonally mustered and desultorily equipped men serving under capricious feudal lords, the military forces of newly unified Spain were transformed into the heavily armed and celebrated <u>Tercios</u> permanently serving under a unified command.

Because of its peculiar historical rhythm and Islamic ingredients, it has become a cliché to say that Spain is less "European" than its neighbors. Yet one may also argue with Julián Marías that in their extraordinary fervor to be European and Christian rather than Oriental and Islamic the Spanish are in a certain sense also more European than other nations.[7]

In comparison to the Spanish, the slower and calmer life of other medieval Europeans is understandable. After all, the latter had no other apparent choice but to be Christian. Culturally speaking, for them the Christian life was a heritage, not a choice. In the case of the Spanish, however, their very condition as Europeans and Christians was in constant jeopardy. For them it was not simply a matter of passively receiving the Christian faith generation after generation but of reaffirming it in the face of the adversary. What was a given for other Europeans was for Spaniards an act of courage and defiance.

It is true that other Europeans—a relative few—fought in the Crusades against Moslem foes, but these sporadic expeditions had a certain air of unreality about them. Hence the tragic "Children's Crusade," for instance, that ended in the death or enslavement of several hundred infants. For most Europeans the enemy, like the fabled lands they occupied, was improbably distant and mysterious. Furthermore, the very enmity between them was too abstract to sustain the prolonged struggles characteristic of the Spanish Reconquest. The Crusaders lacked the passions of proximity. For other Europeans rescuing the Holy

Land was a desirable ideal, yet in the last analysis one they could—and did—safely live without. On the other hand, it would have been unthinkable for the Spanish to forego the Reconquest. For they would have ceased to be Christian and what amounted to the same thing, to be Spanish.

C. Reinterpreting the Renaissance?

There was no Renaissance, not if we understand the term in its usual sense as a break with the medieval past. What we call the Renaissance was the culmination of trends that had been developing for a thousand years.

Unlike the end of the Classical age which saw the rise of a new religion, new artistic motifs, new languages, and the emergence of new peoples on the stage of history, the outstanding features of the period we call the "Renaissance" were continuity, enhancement, and intensification of preexisting modes. In art, for instance, the motifs were unchanged since medieval times but important advances in perspectives and techniques occurred. Perhaps the Renaissance could best be described as innovation within an established tradition. It did not break with the medieval past but coaxed it to fruition.

As for Spain, it has been called "the country without a Renaissance," and we saw earlier how Enlightenment thinkers referred to it as a "medieval" land. It is true that Spain did not experience the abrupt transitions from medieval life we have come to associate with the so-called Renaissance. For example, the gothic style persisted in Spain and the Hispanic Empire until well into the sixteenth century, medieval motifs continued in painting, and the ballad style of poetry (<u>Romances</u>) has survived throughout the Hispanic world to the present day. Yet this preservation of traditional ways did not hinder the introduction of new styles: Italian verse, humanism, new artistic trends, a different kind of monarchy, a new military structure etc.

The abruptness with which the changes we call the Renaissance occurred in other parts of Europe and the smoothness of its inception in Spain suggests that it was the stimulus of Spain that roused other countries out of their immemorial tranquility. Consider these circumstances. At the end of the fifteenth century, Spain appeared on the European horizon as a new species of political reality. Unified under a monarchy that was no longer simply the *primus inter pares* of medieval times but the effective head of a state that pursued a coherent national policy, Spain was the first modern nation, not one of the last as is generally assumed today. There is abundant evidence that other Europeans were startled, and neighboring kings alarmed by the universal Spanish presence. More than a century later Frances Bacon, for instance, marveled that Spain could direct the fortunes of an empire larger than Rome's with so few men and resources.[8] No wonder we can discern a certain rush by "Renaissance" Europe to discard its medieval paradigms in art and governance, for it was quickly readjusting to the phenomenon of unrivaled Spanish power and accomplishment.

Johan Huizinga writes that Erasmus and his followers understood the term "renaissance" in its literal Christian meaning of "rebirth." At the most fundamental level this meant the individual spiritual rebirth that Christ himself taught. Probably too much has been made of the worldly and pagan dimensions of the Renaissance. Huizinga goes on to describe Erasmus—and to a lesser extent Aretino and Castiglione—as "... one over whose Christian sentiment the sweet gale of Antiquity has passed."[9] But at another level Erasmus and other humanists were reacting to what they perceived to be the degraded state of the Christian Church. They looked with alarm—and often with disdain—on the ancient Church dogmas, and they were at odds with the heavy-handed and absolute authority of the ecclesiastical orders. They sought an elegant simplification of Christianity through a greater textual rigor of the Holy Scriptures.

But here we find one of the great ironies of that age. Although unalterably Catholic—witness the martyrdom of Sir Thomas More and Erasmus's resistance to Martín Luther's proposals—by making the Scriptures universally accessible and calling into question the exegetical criteria of the Scholastics, the great humanists foreshadowed the Protestant reforms that were to break the unity of Western Christendom. Ironically, their most obvious Renaissance legacy was not the return of pagan Antiquity but the advent of Protestantism.

The age we call the Renaissance saw stupendous advances. The circumscribed, finite space of medieval art and life, the <u>finis terrae</u> and the <u>non plus ultra</u> of Classical and medieval mankind gave way to infinite perspectives in art and to the real geographical dimensions of the world. Here Iberia excelled. For to the Spanish and Portuguese of the fifteenth and sixteen centuries the world revealed perhaps for the first time its true geographical and human proportions and possibilities.

But these spectacular triumphs and discoveries may cause us to overlook certain essential failures of that age. Consider the main one: the collapse of the humanistic and Christian enlightenment that Erasmus and the other great human proposed. Their hopes for a universal renewal of the Christian faith were dashed by the wave of nationalistic resentments and

Protestant reforms. Furthermore, the humanists continued to write mostly in Latin precisely at a time when the printing press was converting the national languages into powerful instruments of religious ferment, literary creativity, and nationalist sentiment. Consequently, the most enlightened minds of the age were perhaps the slowest to react to the growing spirit of violence. Huizinga says of Erasmus, "[He] perhaps never quite realized how much his philological—critical method must shake the foundations of the Church."[10] Instead of a literal "rebirth," therefore, the hermeneutical methods and erudition of the humanists made available to less prudent men the instruments that destroyed their grand ideal and would soon drag Europe into a hateful conflict to which many contributed but nobody controlled.

Certain important distinctions can be noted in the case of Spain. In the first place, the religious divisions that plagued Northern Europe had only a minimal resonance in Iberia, and, as we saw earlier, the same is true of the superstitious hysteria and terror of the later "witch hunts."

A third feature, the Spanish language itself, is less apparent but certainly no less relevant in this Renaissance context. Unlike the Germanic countries of Northern Europe where Latin was truly a foreign tongue, in Spain and other Romance-speaking lands if not entirely understandable, at least Latin was not wholly incomprehensible. Over the centuries Medieval Latin had been so significantly influenced by its derivative tongues—and vice versa—that if not transparent, it was at least "translucent" to the speakers of Romance languages.

Furthermore, the Spanish language not only remained steadily consistent but also achieved a remarkable expressiveness very early in its development. Practically any educated contemporary Spanish speaker can read the <u>Cantar de Mío Cid</u> or <u>Las siete partidas</u> of Alphonse the Wise and the various <u>Fueros</u>, or city charters, written in the thirteenth century. The fourteenth-century Book of Good Love (<u>El libro de buen amor</u>) is fully accessible to the modern reader.

Compare this linguistic continuity to the development of French or English. The <u>Song of Roland</u> (<u>La Chanson de Roland</u>) (twelfth century) is simply incomprehensible without a specialized knowledge of old French, and the English of Chaucer is nearly as impenetrable even though it dates from the fourteenth century. And as for "English" epic <u>Beowulf</u>, it is not written in English but in Germanic Anglo-Saxon from which modern English derives only in part.

Thus, the linguistic isolation from Latin that once characterized many uneducated Europeans has been replaced in modern times by the disjunctive evolution of their own tongues. Great portions of the medieval and early modern legacy of France and England are all but linguistically inaccessible to modern readers. On the other hand, with scarcely any need of notes or translations Spanish speakers can savor and master the earliest manifestations of their culture. This is yet another dimension of the greater human depth and richness of Hispanic culture alluded to in the preceding chapter. Naturally, whether or not they choose to exploit this richness or to ignore it is altogether another matter.

Most likely this linguistic continuity has much to do with the smoother transition in Spain from the medieval to the modern age. It is probably true, as writers such as C.S. Lewis and historian Rosenstock-Huessy claimed, that modern man still bears within himself the submerged cultural encoding of the Middle Ages. For the Spaniard, however, it is not a matter of concealment but of transparency. This is why Spanish history is characterized by a high degree of clarity—provided the story is truly Spanish and not a tale of something else.

D. THE HEBREW VISION OF THE FUTURE

Let me comment here on the Hebrew vision of the future so as to clarify the points on European futurism that we have been examining. This reason seems clear enough: Christian and European cultures are radically indebted to the Hebrew understanding of the world. This was especially true with the advent of Protestantism with its greater reliance on the Semitic elements of the Christian faith.

To begin with, the Hebrews looked not so much toward the future as through it to what lay beyond. If Europe sought fulfillment in future time, the Hebrew looked to the apocalyptic consummation of time itself.

Far from understanding history in the modern Hegelian sense, i.e., as the evolutionary unfolding of something implicit and possible from the beginning, the Hebrews, and to a lesser degree perhaps their medieval and modern Jewish descendants, saw it as a provisional record that would disappear without a trace when God willed it. Although terribly concrete and urgent, in the final analysis the Hebrew world was unsubstantial. Strictly speaking, to the Hebrew mind the world was not truly real but only a stage on which the divine drama was being acted out. The Hebrew existed physically in the material world, but spiritually he lived on another plane defined by the Law and the Covenant.

To the Hebrew mind only the Divine was truly real. This

meant that the foundation of personal reality did not cohere with the hoary European and Western formulas of the real—*ousia*, being, idea, reason—but depended on a Covenant through which the Hebrew sought to propitiate the Divine will. Far from existing as an autonomous reality, human life was a contingency of God.

From the Hebrew point of view, therefore, it would have been a vain and arrogant effort to attempt to ground life and thought in the Greek notion of *Logos* with its subsets of logic, discourse, reason, and rationalism. (Only after Saint John equated the concept with the Second Person of the Divine Trinity did it transcend its Greek origins and become the quickening principle of Christian theology.) The Hebrew would have dismissed as folly the foundational Greek and Western assumption that there exists a coherence (an adequatio) or at least a no less defining incoherence in times of intellectual crisis between the structure of the cosmos and the coordinates of the human mind.

European peoples, like the Greeks before them, came to believe that it was possible to make sense of the world because, as believers confessed, God had created it, or, as the skeptics held, because it was susceptible either to reason or its alter ego, irrationality. In either case, reality was compatible with human intellect, for faced with a seemingly incoherent world the Classical or European thinker could always consign it to logical absurdity, the final refuge of the rationalistic mind.

For the Hebrew, on the other hand, the world was formally incomprehensible from the start precisely **because** God had created it, and as such it was subject exclusively to the Divine will. The righteous Hebrew had implicit faith in God, but unlike the European mode of rational discourse it was precisely this faith that justified and nourished Hebrew doubts about the material world. The more the Divine transcended the mind of the Patriarchs and Prophets, the deeper and sturdier their faith. Think of Job and Abraham.

Even though at the dawn of the Christian era late Classical man could say <u>Credo quia absurdum est</u> (I believe because it is absurd), this profession of faith still reflected a process of rationalism in the Greek and European mode. For unlike the ingenuous attitude of the ancient Hebrew Patriarchs and Prophets, this statement of Christian belief presupposes a disillusionment arrived at by dialectical rationalism. For things to be labeled absurd they must first be compared to other things that are not.

Through Christianity Europeans inherited the Hebrew belief in the divine Creation and eschatological consummation of the secular age, concepts that were alien to the Greek mind. But also through the teachings of Christianity a belief arose in the possible fulfillment of this world and time. It is true that early Christians often scorned this life, but Christ himself did not. In declaring his great mission to mankind, "I am come that ye might have life and have it more abundantly," Christ does not defer our happiness until the next life but promises that our blessings will commence here and now in this one. The Beatitudes begin with the words, "blessed are... "not "blessed will be..."

E. IMPLICATIONS OF THE CHRISTIAN WORLD VIEW

The European conversion to Christianity led in time to a double-leveled understanding of the future, and to a dual hope. Without surrendering their hope in the trans-future world, by the end of the Middle Ages it is clear that Christians had come to believe also in a better life in the earthly future. From this perspective the great outpouring of creative genius, energy, and optimism we know as Renaissance humanism may be understood in the broadest sense as the Christian restoration of the possibilities of secular life.

But this splendid paradigm did not hold. For no sooner did European Christianity start to recover its secular, humanist dimensions than efforts began to ridicule the supernatural hopes of man. Religious skepticism was already evident as early as the Renaissance, though it would not become intellectually fashionable until two centuries later during the age of Enlightenment. Thomas Nashe (1567-1601), for example, a contemporary of Shakespeare, describes the skeptics of his day in Christ's Tears over Jerusalem (1593): "Most of them, because they cannot palpabrize [touch] or feel God, confidently and grossly discard Him." He adds: "Stoutly they refragate [contravert] and withstand, that the firmament is not His handiwork, nor will they credit one generation telling another of His wonders." [11] During that same era an anonymous work circulated (for a time erroneously attributed to Italian poet Bernardo Accolti), De Tribus Impostoribus Mundi (On the Tribe of World Impostors), in which the claims of Christ, Moses, and Mohammed are refuted. Nashe himself, though a professed believer of sorts, was not only grossly anticlerical but poisonously anti-Puritan and anti-Calvinist.

We have advanced this premise: **at its core the European condition consists of an unusually acute inclination toward the future as potentiality or possibility**. To be European has meant historically to be projected—or perhaps drawn—toward the future in the pliable or malleable definition we have given it.

But this description is incomplete. For we must understand

this futuristic projection not as a single trajectory but as several of varying intensity, range, and duration. Some are short-lived and trail away to indifference or give way to others that correspond to greater enthusiasm or urgency. Others, however, more closely linked to our condition, may last an entire lifetime, disappearing perhaps during long stretches of time but reemerging during moments of greater personal authenticity.

This protean sketch makes sense only in a context of human freedom, for without it we cannot speak meaningfully of authenticity at all. But freedom itself must also be understood in a projective and dynamic way. It is never merely an extraneous quality, much less an abstract "right," for it comes into existence only as the free movement toward our personal destiny. In other words, freedom exists only insofar as we dare to live freely. The modern "freedoms" guaranteed by statute and constitution are in reality only the precondition of freedom, which begins where they stop. (And the modern state infringes more than we realize on "natural" freedoms; for instance, by telling its citizens where and when they can cross a street or park an automobile, by ordering them to inoculate and educate their children, and in many countries by forcing them to vote.) For this reason, we must not assume that freedom is limited to the chance to choose between several options. It may include such choices, but freedom really flourishes only after we have made our initial selection. We are never freer than when we commit ourselves without reservation—Quixotically, as it were—to what, or whom, we truly love and serve.

But the choice we make and the freedom that comes into play when we do so, does not necessarily imply an initial plurality of alternatives. There may be only one way open to us. Where, then, is freedom in these circumstances? Is it not in the free ratification of our destiny? Freedom occurs when we say "no" to mere fate and "yes" to our destiny. Naturally, it is possible to deny or reject even the unavoidable, but the price we pay is inauthenticity of life and the forfeiture of freedom.

This projective and necessarily free condition in which history and the pliable future converge in creative synthesis has opened to the European way of life an unprecedented range of vital possibilities. What is more, in this futuristic predisposition the European finds the most radical fidelity to himself, that is, to his destiny. And in passing, here he discovers also some of the greatest risks, for with the increase of possibilities comes an increase in the range and forms of possible inauthenticity, just as the growth of general knowledge also extends the parameters of individual ignorance. The result is our common modern experience: today we know less and less about more and more, or as "experts," more and more about less and less.

Obviously, these commentaries on the creative vision of the future should not be understood as manifestations of escapist or unsubstantial idealism. Like everyone else, Europeans have no choice but to live in the present regardless of what we have been calling their futuristic inclinations. But theirs is a present permeated or tinged with future possibilities, and this means that to an extraordinary degree European life appears incomplete and unfinished. In this sense, we must make our life and create our own story. Ortega said that we are the novelists of ourselves, and in the struggle—the agony—to complete our uncertain story Unamuno found the paradoxical wellsprings of life and faith. Later Existentialist writers such as Sartre made a fetish of this obligation to forge the content and meaning of otherwise empty human existence.

Unlike the great majority of cultures that boast of their definitive way of life and the uncontested hegemony of the past, European man has no choice but to surpass his history in the problematic task of inventing his life. Paradoxically, the current objections raised to "Eurocentrism"—the so-called "rule of dead white men"—are themselves a crude manifestation of the fundamental European imperative. For of all the cultures we know about, the European is surely the most likely to question the authority of the dead and to supersede their mandates.

The European way of life is, therefore, impossible and unthinkable without freedom. But we should not rush to assume that freedom is equally paramount in other cultures. Those societies in which human life is predetermined by tradition or ideology tend to look upon personal freedom as a public nuisance and often a subversive threat to order. In primitive societies, for instance, where life unfolds according to immemorial custom, the notion of personal freedom hardly exists at all. Yet as if to compensate for this lack neither are these societies beset by the sort of apprehensive uncertainties about life that in one way or another weigh on the person of European roots. Exposed to a thousand dangers and superstitious terrors, primitive man remains at the same time exempt from the existential *angst* that disturbs the European, and Heidegger's insistence to the contrary, it is unlikely that elemental man spends his life raising questions about metaphysical being. More likely his consuming concern is finding his daily bread.

Perhaps this helps to explain the curious nostalgia or envy—often with overtones of self-recrimination and societal reproach—that grips persons of European roots as they observe or study cultures that we once called "primitive." In these moments of discouragement and uncertainty about life and weighed down by the futuristic and ontological responsibility for the world, European peoples experience the existential urge to flee to a simpler life. If the unthinkable sin of the primitive consists of turning his back on nature, the constant temptation of the European is return to the natural world.

I must correct something l said earlier. I wrote that European man lives in a present "tinged" with the possible future. Now I must also admit that the image causes us to think of a temporal usurpation, a utopian subordination of the present to the future. It is true that utopianism has long been a feature of the European way of life, but this is not what I meant. Instead, it is a matter of examining the "anatomy" or consistency of the present time.

In European culture the anticipation or angle of inclination toward the possible future is so pronounced that much of the present consists of what we could call its "ideal quadrant." If in other cultures the *pondus*, the *gravitas*, is yesterday, which has a decelerating or braking action on life, in European life the present moves several degrees toward the future. For the European to live today is also to live in one way or another from tomorrow's perspective. Therefore, because the future is the dimension of life the European characteristically associates with hopeful anticipation (rendered more concisely by the Spanish term *ilusión* mentioned earlier), it is the region of happiness. Naturally, happiness is inseparable from the possibility of unhappiness. All people experience moments of happiness and pain, but because of the unique futuristic inclination of European life, the gamut of these experiences is noticeably more complex than in the majority of other cultures.

No wonder, then, if we look beneath the artistic and cultural nuances and the corresponding critical theories characteristic of each era, we discover that European realism always exhibits ideal dimensions that set it apart from other conceptions of the real: the concreteness of Chinese life, the fatalism of the Moslem, or the obscure magical realism of primitive man. For European peoples, regardless of how real the world appears, it never loses entirely its transcendent dimensions. The new is always possible; innovation is an ever-necessary option. And as for personal reality, to be human is to lack a definitive, limiting nature; being consists in never being in a finished, perfected state. To put it in more human terms, to be a person is to strive to become more so. Hence the strange concepts of vital *dynamis*, of "progress" and "evolution" long since formalized as typical European doctrines and ideologies but heretical and alien heresies when viewed in the light of other intuitions of the real. For this reason, Hegel is the prototypical European thinker, and—to paraphrase Voltaire—if he had not lived, probably it would have been necessary to invent him anyway.

From this perspective, the series of alternating, opposing paradigms in which European art and thought have been conceived since Classical times—idealism/realism, mysticism/rationalism, subjectivism/objectivism, classicism/romanticism, etc.—must be understood at a deeper level as complementary dimensions of the same species of reality. Whenever attempts have been made to abolish one side or the other of this dynamic equation—idealistic, lyrical, mystical, or aesthetic on the one hand, or concrete, tangible, measurable, and scientific on the other—the pendulum of European inspiration has swung in the other direction and balance is restored. In history the ignored real or ideal dimensions of life spend their exile preparing for return and revenge.

It turns out, therefore, that classicism, romanticism, and assorted realisms cannot be reduced to localized artistic or intellectual movements, that is, to the formal movements and schools that bear the name. Instead, they are recurrent and permanent predispositions, or better, acquisitions of the European spirit. Neither do they simply repeat themselves. History is never the same history, and hence our image of the swinging pendulum is inaccurate. This means that the idealistic, lyric, mystical, and romantic tendencies that became predominant in late eighteenth and early nineteenth-century European art, music, and letters can hardly be limited to the few decades of the so-called "Romantic Age." On the contrary, in one form or another these features have been appearing in European life since it first began to take form in the Middle Ages. In Spain, for instance, a common idealistic thread ties the chivalric ideals, ballads, and art of the Middle Ages to Renaissance humanism, to Baroque artists, to the Mystics, to the Romantics, and to the longing for ideal beauty and grandeur that marked the generations of 1898. Far from simply completing the abortive Romanticism of their grandparents, the generations of 1898 drank from a current that flowed from much earlier times. For once again they proclaimed in their own inimitable way the rights of ideal reality.

Once they are expressed as art and thought and have been assimilated into human experience, these ideal dimensions of reality exhibit the characteristic ontological persistence of all real things. For this reason, European people do not cease being who they have been historically. In varying ways, they continue to be at once medieval and enlightened, materialist and idealist, realist and romantic, lyrical and rationalist, democrat and elitist, revolutionary and royalist. When seen from this angle, culture is the repertory of ways of being which form the ideal space and vital richness of human life. To forego any of them is to surrender dimensions of hard-won humanity. For if humanity is a creation, then it is also a conquest over the natural realm. As Arnold put it, "Man begins, know this, where nature ends."

F EUROPE AND THE WEST

Our terminology has been imprecise. We have spoken exclusively in terms of Europe, yet today Europe and the West have converged and become synonyms. Strictly speaking, European civilization is no longer limited to the northern shores of the Mediterranean but instead through migrations, expansions, and incorporations it has come to be the West, primarily, Europe and America.

Here we cannot overlook the fact that Hispanic America, not North America as we generally assume today, was the first "Western" expansion of Europe and that it retains its essential Western character—language, religion, law, medicine, institutional structures, etc.—despite efforts to reassign it to the so-called "third world." **For the better part of a century Hispanic America has listened mostly to those who glorify its aboriginal elements. Perhaps now the time is coming when these republics will also reclaim their original Western destiny.**

The predominance of Western civilization has grown to such dimensions that today a network of satellite nations exists in which, for better or worse, a wide spectrum of Western life prevails. Such is the case in science, technology, parliamentary politics, academies, universities, economic structures and policies, fashions, sports, amusements, food, and the use of a lingua franca such as French or English.

But here we must be cautious and think twice about claims of a culturally unified world. For although these features of Western life bear the same name, often they function in very different ways in non-Western societies. For example, non-Western "universities" are hardly universal but in most cases the servants of parochial or national interests. For where the Greek mind did not penetrate intellectual curiosity for its own sake and for disinterested science did not take root and though half-heartedly imitated today is still not fully understood in many parts of the world.

Probably nothing shows Western hegemony more clearly than the vehemence with which many non-Westerners oppose its influences. But so far this hostility has proved to be as vain as it is destructive to the cultures it claims to protect. To defend any culture is to alter it forever. As they always have been, Western ways have proven again to be imperialistic. Today many countries are becoming hybrid states, that is, societies with a reduced nucleus of native traditions adapted to aggressive Western practices.

Paradoxically, in recent decades we have seen that Europe itself has displayed some of these same resentments against its offspring America. As the futuristic tendencies reach extreme proportions in America—especially in the United States, a land of extremes but an enemy of extremists—as it seemed to become more European than Europe itself, the Western flight toward the future accelerates accordingly, causing a generalized uneasiness in the European spirit.

But most likely the root of this discontent is not only, or even principally, simply a difference of historical acceleration, a theme masterfully treated by Ortega. For a century and a half beginning with the writings of de Tocqueville and Crèvecoeur Europeans admired America whose "common man" portrayed by Walt Whitman and others became a prototype for nineteenth-century European thinkers, just as the "noble" American savage had been an idealized human type for eighteenth-century Europe. Throughout most of its existence America's most admired exports were images of unique human types, not its mechanical artifacts, as we tend to think.

Nowadays it seems that Europe has become uneasy over the American tendency to convert clear purpose into complex process and to embrace change for its own sake and without good reason, or at least without a convincing reason. Paradoxically, this institutionalized change occurs when there is a dimming of the futuristic vision that has always characterized European and Western civilization. For where there is high purpose and brimming enthusiasm bureaucracy cannot flourish. Yet the bureaucrat and the utopian easily tolerate each other, united as they are by their indifference to the future, that is to say, to their future possibilities.

G. FORMS OF 'NATIONALISM AND PATRIOTISM

As the first European nation in the modern meaning of the term, Spain was born without the sense of appositional or confrontational nationalism that later would characterize Europe. Although Castile led the Spanish Reconquest, it never tried to forge Spain in its image by "Castilianizing" non-Castilian lands. Consequently, it never became a country, and at first was not even a kingdom. Ortega said that "Castile made Spain and then dismantled it." To which Sánchez-Albornoz responded that "Castile made Spain and Spain dismantled Castile." For his part, Julián Marías wrote "Castile made itself into Spain," adding that "Castile dedicated itself not to making Spain but to making itself into Spain." [12]

Américo Castro makes much of the foreign origin of the very word *"español"* (Spanish), which seems to have originated in Provence. But without subscribing to the dubious conclusion he draws from this fact—the backwardness of the Spanish Christians etc.—it highlights something we need to consider here. To begin with, this apparent lapse may best be explained not by the supposed ignorance or carelessness of medieval Iberians but by their historical condition at the time.

Early medieval Spaniards thought of themselves simply as Christian in opposition to other people who were not. Jiménez de Rada so defines those who struggled against the Moslems and explains the reason for their resistance in Asturias: **Christiani nominis aliquam scintillam conservare. Saraceni enim totam Hispaniam occupaverant** (to preserve some spark of the Christian name, for the Moslems had occupied all of Spain). [13]

Here we find one of the keys to Spanish history. The subordination of regional Castilian interests to the ideal of a unified Spain infused the protracted struggle we call the Reconquest with a certain altruistic tone—with as many lapses and deviations as one may wish to point out.

This attitude, never completely eradicated in modern times, was to condition all later versions of Spanish nationalism and patriotism. Unlike other varieties of European and Western patriotism which were rooted in diverse nationalisms and characterized by jingoistic exclusivism, in a word, by nationalistic chauvinism, the original Spanish equivalents arose from a Catholic and Christian inspiration. Consequently, only in moments of national weakness and spiritual drift have the Spanish assumed xenophobic postures—the end of the seventeenth century, the first years of the 1898 era, etc. On the other hand, in other eras Spanish life has exhibited an altruistic, hospitable attitude of openness and good will. To cite an illustrious example, Cervantes, who was irrevocably rooted in his Spanish condition and without the slightest resemblance to what might be called a "citizen of the world" in the modern cosmopolitan meaning, nevertheless was humanely tolerant and appreciative of Frenchmen, Italians, Englishmen, Moslems, and all cultural shadings of Iberians.

Commenting on this innate Spanish generosity of spirit, Ángel Ganivet pointed out that while there have been civil wars in Spain, almost no wars of aggression have occurred. Unification occurs in eras of peace, division in times of war.[14]

Not surprisingly, therefore, these respective Spanish and European versions of patriotism have evolved along different lines. Those nourished by nationalistic concepts tend to culminate in exclusivistic attitudes within and hostile postures toward foreigners. But this unconditional identification with the fatherland, which in modern times has been considered to be the highest national virtue, often turns out to be a marker of the limitations of a people. Because of its hermetic nature this kind of patriotism usually proves incapable of a humane and inviting national agenda. It does not readily permit those outside the constitutive racial, cultural, or linguistic paradigms to collaborate as equals in the collective enterprise but consigns them to secondary roles as subjected, "minority" peoples. The more fervently this species of patriotism embraces its purist principles, the more dangerous it becomes to both internal minorities and neighboring countries. Think of the imperialistic aggressions and the presumptions of racial and cultural superiority that have characterized Germany, Great Britain, and the United States in eras of patriotic apotheosis.

Because of its inherently belligerent nature, this jingoistic patriotism—practically the only variety still extant in today's world—shows a natural affinity for aggressive modern ideologies. Perhaps this is why in the twentieth century the virulent patriotism captured in such expressions as "German Fatherland" and "Mother Russia" was expressed—and as often concealed—in fascist and Marxist phraseology. For the most part these harsh totalitarian forms have subsided, yet there are worrisome symptoms that the hyper democracies that replaced them as world powers may also be susceptible to another order of ideological absolutism.

The objection may be raised that history disproves what I have just written about the native altruism of Spanish patriotism. It is true, as we have seen earlier, that since the days of Feijóo and Jovellanos in the eighteenth-century Spanish isolationism has been endlessly debated. Ortega, for instance, lamented the dual tendencies toward what he called Spanish "particularism" and "tibetanization" and similar themes on Spanish "Europeanization" and "Hispanization" abound in the writers of 1898. In an earlier generation, novelists Galdós and Pereda debated, respectively, the merits of European enlightenment and traditional Spanish values. But the fact that most writers perceived national isolationism to be regrettable obviously means that they did not consider it to be the normal Spanish condition. Certainly, there are countries—Tibet, for example— which seek isolation as the condition of interna] peace and wellbeing. But Spain is not one of them. History places this fact in indisputable evidence: in isolation Spain has always felt diminished, stagnant, anguished.

Let us repeat a point so as to make others: within the common Europeanism it shares with its European neighbors Spain has lived by a different rhythm. For instance, just as it achieved Christian unity after nearly a thousand years of struggle with Islam—eight centuries of contention against <u>Al-Andalus</u> and Africa and yet another against the more aggressive Turkish version, the first divisions in Western Christendom were beginning in Northern Europe. In its wars against the Protestants—tragic like all fratricidal conflicts—Spain fought with the same intensity with which it had defended the Christian and Catholic cause against the Moslems. Julián Marías describes the Spanish attitude with these comments: "When the division came about, Spain felt itself necessarily linked to the one Church which it had fought for against the Moslems until it became what it had to be. The Reformation was not simply a critical movement, not even a heresy within the Christian community, but a separation, a rupture. For Spain to have accepted it would have seemed not only a sin against the Faith but unfaithfulness to the Spanish condition, a desertion of the extremely long historical endeavor in which she had come to be herself." [15]

To Marías's commentary I would add only one significant detail. If it would have been an act of infidelity to God and herself for Spain to sanction the Protestant cause, for the Protestant reformers the opposing proposition was probably no less compelling and nationalistic. Of course, the "protests" that ostensibly gave rise to Protestantism—the sufficiency of Divine Grace, Papal authority, the polemics concerning free will and predestination, etc.—were theological in nature and grave disagreements soon separated it from Catholicism. But beyond these questions, Protestantism must also be seen at another level as a great nationalistic awakening among the peoples of Northern Europe. And this brings us to the question of different species of nationalism.

We have already seen how the Spanish condition derived from its ancient Catholic and European "calling" in the face of the Moslem adversary. This means that Spanish nationalism arose originally as an indistinguishable subset of the will to be Christian. Hence also the patriotism *sui generis* we saw earlier.

These traits become clearer if we contrast them with their modern Protestant equivalents. Unlike the Spanish nationalistic sentiment, which is organically rooted in the Catholic condition and therefore necessarily universal in its true state, Protestantism tends to derive culturally—it is important to stress the term—from inward-looking nationalism to which it appeals in moments of crisis and apotheosis. Hence the original close identification of certain branches of Protestantism with the regions, times, countries, ethnicities, and languages of origin— the "Anglican" Church of England, the Lutherans of Germany and other Germanic countries, the Quakers and Amish, "Southern" Baptists and other American sects, etc.

From a sociological point of view, we see that the parameters of Protestant religiosity require a civil and political structure of high moral and ethical standards. In Protestant societies the moral missteps of its leaders have been taken very seriously, for these shortcomings directly affect the very matrix of faith, which depends on decent public order. In short, the Protestant faith presupposes a civic faith. Hence the admirable civil aptitude of the Protestant citizenry in a virtuous public climate and no less their disturbing tendency to conform to perverse regimes. Far unlike Catholicism, Protestantism lacks an effective, united, universal voice. Thus, it must trust to the stability and essential benevolence of the State. No wonder, then, the Protestant anguishes over transgressions that in cultures with Catholic roots would amount at most to embarrassing trivialities that in no way—or so it may seem—affect the foundations of public order and decorum. In sum, for the Protestant, citizenship and faith support each other and are inseparable, while for the Catholic good citizenship is a consequence of a primary faith.

As an island is defined by the surrounding sea, so Spanish nationalism and patriotism are a function of its Catholic history. The Spaniard is no less a citizen or a patriot than his Protestant counterpart, but historically speaking, unlike the Protestant, he is a citizen because he is Catholic first. To put it another way, Spanish nationalism is filtered through a prior Catholicism, whereas Protestantism is distilled through a prior nationalism. Thus while the Protestant serves God by serving his country, the Spaniard serves his country by serving God. Perhaps this is why Antonio Machado has Juan de Mairena declare that "Spain has never fought because of national or racial pride, but rather because of human pride and love of God, which are one and the same."[16]

H. SPAIN AND THE MODERN MIND

For several centuries Spain adhered to this Catholic nationalism, often subordinating national interests to its vision of a pan-Christian unity, the *Universitas Christiana* we saw earlier.

But as modern nationalism intensified between 1650 and 1700 Spain abruptly abandoned the European and world stage, withdrew from its neighbors, and began a long period of isolation that strictly speaking still has not completely ended. Why? How does one explain this strange behavior by a nation that perhaps more than any other established the primary conditions that made the modern world possible in the first place?

There is no dearth of explanations for the Spanish withdrawal and relative decline. Volumes have been written about the famous Spanish "decadence," the inept regimes of the last Hapsburg monarchs, the weariness and weakness of the Spanish after centuries of struggle, discovery, creativity, and expansion on a scale unparalleled in human history. Yet these explanations, besides being excessively vague to begin with and gainsaid at every point by contradictory facts, explain very little but instead require an explanation. For instance, the transnational and transcontinental Hispanic Empire of "the Spains" (*las Españas*) continued to flourish throughout the era of "decadence."

But as unsatisfactory as Decadence theory turns out to be, there is no denying that peninsular Spain suffered at least a relative decline during this period. At a time when its sister nations were growing demographically and commercially at unprecedented rates, Spain lost population, economic initiatives, and its relative military superiority.[17] Its once feared military *tercios* were no longer invincible as other nations now equaled or surpassed the Spanish in military firepower and might. Economic and agricultural declines coupled with ministerial and monarchical ineptitude—or at least stagnation—caused Spain to lose many of its early advantages over the rising nations of France, Holland, and England.

Yet even during the height—or depth—of so-called Spanish "decadence," the reign of Charles II (1665-1700), the last of the Hapsburg kings, Spain was still a formidable power. An objective assessment of its real capabilities and weight in world affairs only partially supports the conventional premises of Spanish demise. It is commonly supposed, for instance, that with the defeat of the Invincible Armada (1588) Spain ceased forever to be a maritime power. The facts indicate otherwise. Within ten years and before the death of Phillip II (1598) the Spanish had built an even larger fleet and would maintain an impressively large navy throughout the seventeenth and eighteenth centuries. Not until the battle of Trafalgar in 1805 and the defeat of the combined Spanish and French fleets did Spanish naval power suffer a decline that proved to be irreversible during the nineteenth century. Naturally this loss hindered communications among the several "Spains" and the resulting isolation probably was a factor in the breakup and fragmentation of the Empire, although as far as I know this remains a relatively untested hypothesis.

Azorín claimed in Una hora de España (1924) that the Decadence never existed, citing the titanic effort Spain exerted to build thousands of cities, to populate and civilize a continent, and to create a score of Spanish-speaking nations in the process. Later studies by the Duke of Maura Vida y reinado de Carlos II (1942]), Henry Kamen La España de Carlos II (1981), and Julián Marías España inteligible (1985), to name but a few, provide a solid basis for revising the traditional assumptions about the Decadence.

What seems to be beyond question, however, is the lingering phenomenological impact of the Decadence. With or without solid historical validity, the Decadence became an assumption of Spanish history. Marías comments: "What was decisive and of lasting effect was the state of mind of Spaniards and the majority of foreigners, induced to a large degree by the latter in the former. The impression of decadence became fixed in their minds and souls—which was the contrary of what been happening from the advent of the Catholic Kings until the end of the sixteenth century. No even the facts gainsaying decadence could dispel the conviction of its existence and irreversibility."[18]

If the conventional theories about Spanish decline prove to be unsatisfactory, then we must look elsewhere for more substantial reasons. And since we have been reminding ourselves that Spain is in Europe, this means that we must turn to the European causes that radicalized the Spanish and changed the very nature of its foreign policies.

Between 1600 and 1700 the modernization of European life and the final waning of the Middle Ages were in full acceleration If medieval life had been characterized by what we could describe as a belief structure, modernity exhibited a growing reliance on ideation, that is, on ideas. Medieval people had only a negligible impact on their life. (Hence their apparent mental simplicity.) They lived ontologically secure within a firm system, of unquestionable beliefs, including those. centered on religious faith.

As the modern age dawned the reliance on belief as a way of life began to wane. This should be understood precisely, for at first it was not simply a matter of ceasing to believe. In any number of personal cases conscious adherence 'to religious beliefs, for instance, became greater than ever. Witness the vehemence of the Reformers and their followers. Suddenly men rushed forth armed with ideas to defend the beliefs Europeans had taken for granted for a thousand years. But this defense was also an unintended attack on the very beliefs they cherished. For as Ortega argued, beliefs by nature are unconscious assumptions of reality itself. They are like water to a fish: so omnipresent and engulfing that normally we have no inkling of them. Once we become aware of them, they cease to function as the invisible components of our reality but instead appear on the surface of life, thus becoming "superficial" and sooner or later vulnerable to our whims, preferences, and ideas. As I suggested earlier, nothing changes a belief more radically than defending it.

The modern age is as rich in ideas—including their more complex or ephemeral versions: hypotheses, theories, opinions, etc.—as it is poor in beliefs. There is one, however, that until recently has retained its unconscious preeminence: the unquestioned belief in ideas as such, i. e. in their efficacy and right to intellectual supremacy. Modernity rests largely on this odd ideational faith.

We have seen already how Spain retained much of its medieval character without prejudice to its acceptance of the so-called "Renaissance" art and ideas. Moreover, the polemical and belligerent character of Spanish religiosity during the Middle Ages infused it with a proto-modern awareness of its beliefs that differentiated it from other versions of European Christianity. Indeed, it was this feature among others, that allowed Spain to anticipate the modern European ethos.

But this long, almost hereditary defense of the Christian faith also had sensitized the Spanish not only to what they regarded as the excesses inherent in the modern way of thinking, particularly the Protestant Reformation, but also to the need to reinvigorate the core of Catholicism. The Erasmian humanists began with essentially the same premise but with an extra-ecclesiastical bias that won them little support within the Church and, as we have seen, in an indirect manner abetted the Protestant movement more than Catholicism itself. On the other hand, the Spanish launched an energetic movement to reinvigorate the Church from within. The Society of Jesus founded by Ignatius Loyola and his followers (1539) soon became, even granting all its imputed faults, the most effective force within the Church. Almost simultaneously at the Council of Trent (1545-1563) Spanish theologians vigorously resisted the rising schismatic trend toward "national" churches. Instead of a "Hispanic" Church" modeled along the lines of the Protestant "Anglican" or the Catholic "Gallic" counterparts, the Spanish advocated the <u>Universitas Christiana</u>, which if already politically unrealistic by the middle of the sixteenth century was still possible within Catholicism itself.

For reasons that we shall touch on later, Spain soon relinquished its leadership and became defensive and distrusting, reacting—usually negatively—to events rather than directing them. This retrenchment was especially true in philosophy and science. But from the sixteenth to the twentieth century Catholic thought in general and not just in Spain exhibited a distrust of the modern world and a preference for medieval forms ill-suited to deal with the pressures—and especially the ideological temptations—of modern times.

With the advent of Protestantism, the ancient geographical and dogmatic unity of Western Christendom was rent asunder, but as a result a further reduction of the old universality occurred within Catholicism itself. Instead of simply addressing all peoples *urbi et orbi*, now it spoke to its adherents and against the Protestant versions of Christianity. Paradoxically, as early as the sixteenth century, Catholicism itself began to "echo" certain "Protestant" practices, for just as Protestantism depended adversarially on Catholicism for its very existence, so Catholicism soon carne to substantiate its claims to Apostolic legitimacy by polemical comparisons to what it rejected as apostate Protestantism. In short, in protesting against Protestantism, Catholicism itself became somewhat "protestant."

Thus, an adversarial co-dependency between Catholics and Protestants characterized by reciprocal vituperation and intolerance marked the inauspicious advent of modern Western Christianity. It could not have come at a worse time. For just as European science, art, and philosophy were beginning to assume their modern forms, the two antagonistic branches of Western Christianity were pushing each other into postures of dogmatic rigidity and out of the Church's traditional role as the guardian and patron of learning. At first merely estranged and still cast in the moral image of their Christian origin, in time intellectual inquiry and artistic creativity became indifferent, independent, and finally overtly hostile to their original religious matrix.

This hostility toward the new modes in philosophy and science was probably most pronounced in Spain where for the reasons we saw earlier European Catholicism had reached its highest temperature in the fifteenth and sixteenth centuries. But in the seventeenth century Spanish enthusiasm and leadership gave way to disillusionment. The famous Spanish *repliegue*, or retrenchment, was not merely a retreat from Europe and the world, but a profound change of attitude that could best be described as a lack of interest in modernity. In his Cartas eruditas (Erudite Letters) (1742-1760) Father Jerónimo Feijóo relates his astonishment and chagrin upon discovering that his fellow

Spaniards, not foreigners, were responsible for the shameful neglect of worthy Spanish writers in his day.

This loss of enthusiasm constituted the real and abiding Spanish "decadence," for it was first and foremost a decline of human hope. Geographically and physically Spain continued largely unchanged; only the Spanish will to greatness was impaired.

I. IDEAS AND BELIEF

We have seen how the modern world was primarily rooted in a belief in the supremacy of ideas. Perhaps exaggerating a bit, can we not say that a belief in ideas as such constituted modernity's guiding faith? Of course, other eras, most notably Greece, had a genius for ideas, but the modern age excelled in elevating them to the dignity of method, system, and faith.

But for all their vaunted efficacy ideas have the disadvantages of instability and volatility. They can change minds, but minds can also change them. They are at once tyrant and slave to fad and disposition.

The elevation of ideas to modern supremacy created a curious dichotomy that held for centuries. I say for centuries because in recent times the tableau has become blurred, and the clear lines of division are less evident. (Later we shall see how ideas and beliefs have altered the generational cycles in modern times.) Since they were not innate personal traits, ideas had to be learned and transmitted, and this required schools, books, and universities, all of which were traditional male bastions. It is true that European universities had existed for several centuries, but whereas in earlier times their primary function was to transmit traditional knowledge, dogma, and hermeneutical techniques, the modern university inclined—not without considerable controversy—to the creation or discovery of new knowledge using methods based on rationalism and research instead of ancient authority.

A curious educational polarity of the sexes became a defining feature of modernity. On one level, it fell to mothers and the distaff members of the family or community to instill in children the prevailing social mores including manners, decorum, speech, dress, behavior, religious practices, and in the case of daughters in particular, certain vocational skills. For centuries this was the original and only meaning of "education" for most medieval Europeans.

But the modern world of ideas demanded more. Formal intellectual instruction was also needed to complement the primary "education" taught in the home. Hence the rise of modern schools and universities. For their part, men busied themselves with the innovative and fluid realm of ideas, while women were the human agency by which these were either rejected or converted to beliefs.

Regardless of their brilliance, ideas are by nature debatable and polemical and sooner or later likely to yield to more aggressive or attractive alternatives. For this reason, ideas can hardly constitute a harmonious and solid basis of life. To propose to live exclusively within an idea-system is to condemn oneself to unbearable tensions and antagonisms. Yet modern man has tried to live precisely in this way through adherence to one or another of the idea-systems we call "ideologies." (What we call "genius" in the modern world is often nothing more than an outstanding talent for manipulating ideas, whereas its probable equivalent in other ages would be a profundity of wisdom.)

Probably much of the existential anguish of modern life can be traced to this questionable determination to root our life in ideas.

For a long time now, beliefs have suffered from a bad press, associated as they are with the kind of dogmatic intolerance characteristic of the old religious conflicts alluded to earlier. But in reality, beliefs themselves are normally much more forgiving and humane than the abstract thinking and impersonal logic of ideological systems. What normally occurs is that beliefs are enclosed within, and thus distorted by, imperious and impatient ideas. Summoned to serve and defend beliefs, ideas frequently end up usurping them.

Traditionally, beliefs have been the core of woman's life, and until recently this feature has been one of her greatest enchantments. Man, the artful crafter of ideas and dreamer of sublime deeds and fantastic tomorrows, found in belief-anchored woman a different configuration of human life in which the enduring patterns and stability of daily life took precedence over the competitive pace of his idea-driven existence. Furthermore, she seemed to know that the only point of reference and realization of man's far-fetched ambitions was the here and now where she lived. Sooner or later, he must come to her, for the currents of life converged in her. For her, the ideas, theories, and innovative notions of man were valid only insofar as they could be assimilated into everyday life.

In contrast to the volubility of idea-driven man, woman led a calmer life, which is not to say it was necessarily any less painful or penurious. Far from it. Precisely because her life was strengthened by belief, often she could endure more pain and withstand calamity more resiliently than man. If man was absorbed in business, religion, philosophy, history, science, war, or revolution, woman was busy creating and keeping something much more basic and belief-centered: the timeless but timely human home from which zealous man set out to win the world and to which he returned, perhaps worn and disenchanted, in search of consolation far from his male contentions and obsessions.

Now things have changed. Beginning around the time of the Renaissance and with greater acceleration since the Enlightenment, the area of beliefs, the traditional abode of woman, has been progressively shrinking, and with it the social importance of its associated realities and activities. Religious faith, for example, to which we shall return presently, is ever more restricted to certain prescribed areas of life and more or less forbidden access to others.

Perhaps not enough thought has been given to another similar reductionism in feminine life. The deference shown in modem times to publicly circulated ideas and the masculine cast of mind they imply that has come about at the sacrifice of the private world of beliefs has also diminished areas of life traditionally under the dominion of woman. I am not referring to abstract and legal "rights" of "ideational" origin but to actual, belief-centered prerogatives that in a former age woman exercised freely in her home and in multiple private and personal relationships. Ironically, despite modern "feminism," it may be that the prestige of women has never been lower. The more visible woman has become in our day, the less she is esteemed. To put it another way, today woman is less admired, or what amounts to the same thing, less admirable and hence less wonderful and desirable.

Some of the reasons for this decline are obvious. Modern

woman satisfies fewer desires and responds to fewer needs of man and family. Furthermore, many of these responses, which in other times she offered as a prerogative of her condition as a woman, she now views as a distraction from her profession or vocation. Hence the fragility of contemporary marriages and other relationships between the sexes. In addition, many relationships that formerly were largely her responsibility have been assumed by public and social institutions. Consider what has happened to the primary education of children, at least in Western societies.

One could argue that the growing "masculinization" of the modern world through the agency of ideas has had the effect of "defeminizing" Western societies. But even if this is true, the prerogatives wrenched away from women have not, with few exceptions, led to a greater number of privileges for men. Rather the contrary; they represent absolute declines, that is, human losses that diminish both sexes. As woman abandons her traditional belief-centered abode for the idea-based life, she has no choice—or so it seems—but to imitate man, even going so far as to commit the same mistakes and fall into the same vices. In previous centuries woman lived within herself and normally within her home. Today, like man, she is more likely to be beside herself and outside her home, rushing about in a state of competitive agitation far removed from the relative serenity and stabilizing faith that marked the feminine life in former times.

There appears to be no doubt that this progressive abandonment of belief-based life has harmed both sexes. For when woman is not happy, man is desperate. When woman turns her back on her traditional domain, the characteristic restlessness of man increases exponentially. Without the stability of life that woman once offered him, man cannot really be at ease anywhere, and least of all in a house that is no longer a home. On his own, man wanders aimlessly, but almost always toward vice, almost never in the direction of anything good.

But all this occurs within a vast historical context the general outline of which we must now briefly sketch.

J. PROTESTANTISM AND THE MODERN PERSPECTIVE

In the sixteenth century the Protestant theologians—Calvin, Luther, and to some degree the Anglicans—set about to replace the ecclesiastical and canonical order of Catholic Rome with the supreme textual authority of the Holy Scriptures, taking as their ideal the paleo-Christian Church of the Apostolic age. But if theologically they appealed to the authority of the Bible, which recently had been translated into the vernacular languages, reason was the armament with which they attacked Rome and defended themselves in internecine polemics. Reasonable or not, justifiable or not, their dialectical and rhetorical strategy was eminently rational, a fact that later was to assume incalculable importance. Indeed, the several Protestant sects created by the fragmentation of Catholicism went to great lengths to justify textually and rationally their respective theological stands.

Reason functions by means of its created ideas and logical constructs: But we have seen already that ideas are by nature inconstant and subject to overthrow by others of superior construction or appeal. Thus, by abandoning the traditional realm of unquestioned, immemorial beliefs in favor of rationally crafted interpretations and opinions about beliefs, the Reformers loosed an unstable and perhaps uncontrollable "ideational" element in the bosom of Protestant Christianity, and by reflex reaction in Catholicism also. We could say that in this sense ideas were a virus that infected the catholic unity of Western Christendom.

The main problem, apparent from the first and unremedied to this day, was that in principle at least there were as many interpretations of the Scriptures as there were individual believers. Not that the resulting dissensions were normally over obvious cases of hermeneutical divergence. The greatest difficulty was not in surmounting deep differences but in resolving close similarities. Hence the frequent exasperation or satire of non-believers and cynics over what they viewed as sophistry by theologians of every stripe.

From a fund of common or very similar assumptions, an apparently endless and continuing splintering of Protestantism began. None of this could be foreseen at the dawning of rationalistic Protestantism. Indeed, for a time modern rationalism was the loyal servant of the Protestant thinkers, just as Aristotelian logic had faithfully served medieval theology. But if modern reason could be used against Catholicism, it did not take long for it to turn on the new Protestant order. Already in the guise of "methodical doubt" in the hands of Descartes (1596-1650) rationalism quietly began to distance itself from theology. It was Descartes himself who first suggested the notion of hermetic sectors of life when he argued that with respect to the visible and material world, we ought to accept the teachings of modern scientists, for they know more of such things than others. But in the order of truths that deal with faith and personal salvation we must heed what the Church says, for it is closer to the sacred revelations of antiquity. In this realm, unlike the secular, the more ancient the authority the more we should respect it. For perhaps the first time a wedge was driven between the personal world of faith with its eternal hopes and the public world of policy, materiality, and objective fact. This is yet another aspect of the growing abyss between beliefs and rationally-derived ideas.

Protestantism offered no substantial arguments against this understanding of the objective realm. In any case, to the Protestant mind, the physical world, corrupted and spoiled by sin and wickedness, was decidedly secondary. As Leslie Newbigin writes, "It [Protestantism] does not challenge the dominant scientific world—view but keeps, so to speak, a private place for religion within the public world of scientifically understood facts."[19]

Amidst the rising tide of nationalism sweeping over Europe as well as the stunning discoveries made by empirical science—Bacon, Galileo, Copernicus, and later Newton—and the aggressive pressures of rationalistic philosophy ever more removed from the Christian vision of God—Spinoza, Voltaire and other *philosophes* of the Enlightenment—Protestant Christianity chose to withdraw into the world of private faith in order to assure its very existence. Thus bulwarked and in a defensive posture during the Modern Age, it sought to exert some modest influence if not on the public and scientific sectors of life at least on the values of those who by a personal decision accepted its guidance.

This was of course a far cry from the old universal authority of the Church. The residual force of Protestantism soon came to be regarded as one of several moral, philosophical, scientific, and civic understandings of man's place and purpose in the world. In recent times not even the religious realm has been its uncontested domain. Today the Protestant faith has become one among a gamut of available religions and as such without any right to preeminence, much less exclusivity. This is true most of all in nations with a Protestant tradition. Furthermore, not even its most sacred dogmas and principles are spared hostile rationalistic scrutiny. This is why the celebrated dispute between science and religion in modern times is a contest with very unequal rules. For its part, science recognizes no limits to its imperialistic drive, whereas Christianity exposes itself to severe censure if it ventures opinions beyond its circumscribed boundaries.

The notion of "circumscribed boundaries" means that the reductionist criteria of the modern worldview have prevailed over the transrational core of the Christian faith. Naturally it makes no sense to speak of "values" in such a materialistic universe. Or to put it another way, there are as many values as one may wish, for none has any ultimate rational sovereignty. Material things either are, or they are not, but in any case, they are—supposedly—all there is. To the skeptical reductionist, to attribute ethical, moral, or teleological values to material data and phenomena is to fall back into dubious metaphysical and religious contentions.

Within its modest precincts to which it fled to escape modern rationalistic and skeptical aggression, Protestant Christianity assumed as its task the problematic questions of human destiny that science and reason either ignored altogether or dismissed as meaningless suppositions. Yet even as it confronted the enigma of human transcendence, the Protestant theologians had to contend with the prior ravages of rationalism. For since the Enlightenment and particularly since the so-called "higher criticism" of the nineteenth century their task has not been simply a matter of affirming by faith alone the sovereignty of the

Scriptures over the authority of Rome but of justifying the Bible itself according to modern rationalistic criteria. Why, indeed, should one prefer the Bible and not the Koran or the Bhagavad Gita? What rational evidence, if any, is there to support the Biblical claims and facts?

In modern times, bereft of what Peter Berger has called a "Plausibility Structure," that is, a system or fund of beliefs and assumptions that are socially orthodox and unquestionable, all value judgments seem personal and ultimately relative only to circumstances or preferences and without validity beyond the private life of their sponsor.[20]

Whether by free choice or deterministic circumstances, what stands forth is the concept of "credential relativism," or relativity of faith and the tacit denial of absolutes. Voltaire expressed it early and eloquently in *Zaire*:

J'eusse été pres du Ganges esclave des faux dieux, Chrétienne dans Paris, et musulmane en ces lieux. (By the Ganges I should have been the slave of false gods, a Christian in Paris, and a Moslem in this place.)

Thus, a seemingly unbreachable abyss opened between the supposedly relative transcendent beliefs, feelings, and faith of personal life and the objective world of reason, ideas, and impersonal materiality. Separate and conflicting visions or theories of human life developed on each side of the chasm. The Modern Age has been the arena of their struggle for supremacy.

K. CONFLICTING THEORIES OF HUMAN LIFE

The remotest sources of the first theory of man are Hebrew, Greek, and Christian. According to the early Greek thinkers, man is someone who lives mentally as well as bodily. He comprehends the world by enveloping all things with thought and language—the *Logos*. He is free and therefore responsible. He chooses his life ("as the archer chooses his target," said Aristotle). He may be good or evil, happy or wretched, and he desires to go on living forever.

In Greece arose the insatiable human curiosity about the world, and from this unique attitude, so different from anything else on earth, were born philosophy, ethics, aesthetics, science, reason, as well as schools and academies. Unlike the Romans who journeyed to conquer, the Greeks traveled to see and understand truth and beauty. Their conquests were intellectual and aesthetic. (I remarked earlier that in those lands where Greek curiosity took root, universities arose to pursue knowledge for its own sake, whereas in those without a Greek heritage learning has remained largely parochial and utilitarian.)

As Greek and Classical thought merged with Judeo-Christian faith, this anthropology was enriched with the belief that man was created by an effusive act of the Creator and, unlike things, "in His likeness and image." For this reason, man is a person "like" God, i.e., godlike, though not perfect or infinite. As an adopted "child" of God he is brother to other men and women, to all other men and women regardless of their earthly condition, inequalities, and differences. Endowed with intelligence and spiritual understanding, man is able to respond to the Divine Persons of the Trinity and therefore stands apart from things because of his understanding, moral conscience, and filial relationship to the Creator. Furthermore, the difference is not only one of degree or magnitude but of class and kind. For man knows through faith that he is destined to experience a personal resurrection. God will call him by name and lovingly sustain his life forever.

Immortality—and all that refers and attaches to it—is mankind's true "calling" or "vocation" (from *vocare* "to call"). Redeemed from lethal sin by the sacrificial Christ and strengthened by the *Paraclete*, we are restored to freedom and responsible behavior in this world and the next, and as such it is incumbent on us to decide who we are going to be now and forever. Hence the indestructible link between Christian faith and freedom.

This stupendous understanding of human life created a fund of exalted concepts about the human person, among them, respect for the infinite value of human life, inalienable dignity of the individual, freedom of decision and action, and charity and mercy for one's fellow man. With countless lapses and frequent reverses, throughout the long history of European and Western life this elevated Judeo-Greco-Christian vision of humanity created cycle after cycle of art, music, literature, science, civility, statehood, intellectual enlightenment, and individual creativity. Its full realization surpasses the creative channels and expressive modes of any given era. From this surplus flows that boundlessly perfectible future we described earlier as the defining trait of European civilization. It may be that at any given moment of Western history countless people live more or less badly. Their desperation may stir them with revolutionary impatience, but only because they have a vision of something better. At bottom revolution is both a declaration of independence from the past and a violent oath of allegiance to the future. This is why the revolutionary concept probably could have originated nowhere but in European civilization.

For fifteen centuries the teleological ideal of Christian "rebirth" or "renaissance" invigorated European life, serving as an inexhaustible source of culture, learning, and art. For this reason and despite the erroneous anthropological premise that all cultures are—and have been—equal, the Christian-based European ethos is clearly unique, even if that uniqueness can also turn wicked. Ortega claimed that twentieth-century Europe could be equated to science. He may have been right, but we need to remember that modern science carries within it the virtual world perspective from which it arose, just as a sample of genetic material encodes the total organism to which it belongs.

But just as the first theory of man was reaching its zenith in Renaissance humanism, art, and discovery, a "second" theory was preparing to replace it. Apostolic and medieval Christianity regarded the world as both the setting and manifestation of the Divine will. Creation was understood eschatologically as a vast historical and extra-historical movement toward the apocalyptic consummation and apotheosis of time. Human life shared this cosmic destiny, for just as materiality served a higher purpose, so human destiny transcended its undeniable mortality.

Yet with the advent of scientific and philosophical rationalism it no longer seemed necessary to mobilize this divine paradigm. In order to explain the material universe, it sufficed to discover its physical laws. Thus, Mother Nature replaced Father God as the creator of the cosmos and the sustainer of life. According to the new cosmogony, for example, the movement of the planets had nothing to do with "the music of the spheres" or the divine design but was simply the observable functioning of the laws of inertia and gravity. In theory this new understanding meant that the world was knowable by the scientific and rational method. No longer was it a manifestation of a higher power but simply the consequence of the natural laws of cause and effect. This did not necessarily mean the denial of God's existence, for He may still be the author of the operative natural system. But if so, then, unlike the God of Christianity He becomes a "deistic" God, that is, as remote from the workings of the world as He is indifferent to human destiny.

It is a commonplace to say that in shifting allegiance from religious faith to rationalism, Europeans passed from medieval life to the modern age. But this is not quite true, indeed if we press the matter, it is not true at all. Medieval peoples were or could be fully rational and modern peoples either are or can be enormously faithful. It was not a matter of choosing one to the exclusion of the other, which would be an absurdity, but of their relative order and magnitude in human life. At bottom, medieval life and modernity divide over the profound difference between reasoned faith and rational faith. Reason serves to ratify the first but rationality sets the parameters of the second. The hope of modern faith has been to justify itself by becoming rationalistic, whereas medieval faith assumed that it was justified and reasonable to begin with and that Aristotelian reasoning, or logic, was its subservient instrument.

On the other hand, in the seventeenth century—and to an exorbitant degree in the eighteenth—Reason became the true divinity worshiped by thinkers and scientists. As such it soon assumed an absolute sovereignty. It recognized no authority not grounded in fact and boldly confronted the most sacred traditions and dogmas. With supreme petulance—and this describes the likes of Condorcet, Voltaire, d'Holbach, among others—the rationalistic thinkers insisted that no doctrine had the right to oppose what Kant called "the daring to know." In theory every rational person from Adam to us had the same access to the secrets of nature.

Furthermore, the actualization of these rationalistic postulates, which were the cause of unrestrained jubilation among the Enlightenment thinkers, presupposed at the same time an unlimited personal autonomy. If it was true that no dogma could usurp the rights of sovereign reason, it followed that no authority—secular or ecclesiastical—could infringe on the right of the individual to its unrestrained exercise. In fact, any judgmental prerogative belonged to rational enlightenment, not to authority, as Condorcet makes clear: "[Rationalism] was already able to weigh authorities and compare them to one another. In the end it submitted these very authorities to the tribunal of reason."[21]

Hand in glove with this rationalistic prerogative there arose other so-called "natural rights," <u>droits de l'homme</u>, civil rights, etc. Despite an apparent similarity to the privileged status of the religious believer, legal secular rights constituted a new historical phenomenon. Conferred by the State, these secular rights applied only within the territorial boundaries of its government. Unlike the personal, God-given status of the believer which transcended the secular world, the new rights of modern citizenship were "legal" in nature, which meant that they could be declared illegal and void. In any case, they depended on the whims of the State.[22] Alasdair McIntyre argues that it would have been impossible to express the concept of human rights in the Classical and medieval versions of Hebrew, Greek, Latin, and Arabic (<u>After Virtue</u>, p. 123).

The Enlightenment thinkers believed that ignorance of natural law was both the great obstacle to rational progress and the source of all human vices. Hence their emphasis on education, such as Rousseau's Émile. The underlying premises in the new pedagogical theories, including egalitarian principles, the innate goodness of man, and the need to educate the masses, were activated by the radical mandate to discredit established educational institutions, especially the Church, and to some extent, the family. These, or so the philosophes contended, perpetuated obscurantist superstitions and outmoded beliefs.

Of all the available alternatives to these discredited institutions only the new Revolutionary State with its anticlerical and egalitarian tendencies was deemed capable of assuming the task of educating the citizenry. (That the Church retained its pedagogical preeminence in Spain is a fact of enormous historical importance.)

More than a simple displacement of authority was at stake as the old system of beliefs gave way to the aggressive ideas of the Enlightenment. Rather the process involved the creation of the modern paradigm of Western life the most visible characteristics of which were urbanization, state bureaucracy, preponderance of the scientific and rational methods over the earlier humanism, the decline of Christian teleology, and lastly among other factors, the so-called "Industrial Revolution." The latter consisted principally in the transition from a local economy based on individual trades and craftsmanship to an urban market economy sustained by anonymous workers and mass production.

Because modern economics was a creation par excellence of the new value-free rationalism, it owed little to traditional ethics. Lesslie Newbigin summarizes the new market-driven economics: "It was no longer concerned with the purpose of human life. It was no longer about the requirement of justice and the dangers of covetousness. It became the science of the working of the market as a self-operating mechanism modeled on the Newtonian universe."[23]

In passing, we should note that modern industrialization drastically affected family solidarity. Because the father—and lately the mother as well—worked away from the home, this absence not only diminished his authority but also disrupted the transmission of techniques and accumulated cultural knowledge. Consider an example that is not as trivial as it may first seem: the rapid disappearance in Western countries of oral traditions such as stories, songs, games, poetry, sayings, and other forms of folk art and wisdom.

The new rationalism associated with what we have been calling the "second theory" of man had as its justifying principle human welfare and progress, which we may sum up in a single word: happiness. But the happiness the new paradigm offered with one hand, it denied with the other. Medieval man had believed unconditionally that full happiness existed only in the next life. Yet modern rationalism denied a priori any possibility of life after physical death. This meant that the possibilities for happiness were confined to the few years of earthly existence.

It is interesting to note that the Modern Age reversed the traditional roles of youth and old age. Because happiness and the successful life were once associated with distilled wisdom and accumulated knowledge, in earlier epochs the elderly were respected for what they could teach younger generations. But in recent centuries happiness and skill became the prerogative of the young and foolish and the elderly were discarded in the waste bins of life. Instead of the hope of the future, youth became the arbiter and model of happiness today. For their part, the elderly were now uncomfortable reminders of ignominious mortality and a dismaying contradiction of modernity's ideal youthfulness. Hence the pathetic homage paid to youth in our day, particularly by those no longer young.

In the "second" theory of man the Modern State, not God, was the guarantor of human happiness. But it was a generic and impersonal sort of happiness expressed succinctly in John Stewart Mill's formula "the greatest good for the greatest number." Like industrial production, happiness was a mass-produced commodity understood generally as physical and economic welfare. Naturally the State could ill accommodate what we may call here "felicitary deviations" by individuals and it merely tolerated or, latterly, often disapproved of the Christian notion of imperishable personal happiness.

The new mass-produced and generic happiness, corresponding to the second theory of man, was, as almost everybody knows or suspects, no happiness at all on a personal level. For we cannot really be happy knowing that death will soon end it forever. For happiness that ends has another name: unhappiness.

If in the first theory of man he stood only a bit below the angels, in the second theory of human life he rises barely above the apes. He is the homme machine of de la Mettrie, the "human beast" described by nineteenth-century naturalistic writers such as Emile Zola, or perhaps simply a chemical phenomenon or replicable DNA encoding as more recent trends suggest.

These views of man reflect the modern bias toward materialistic reductionism. The assumption is that nothing is fully real until it has been reduced to its components. The parts are more substantial than the whole. Man's physical body is more real than his desires, his psyche, and his soul, and the chemicals that make up his body are even more so.

Expressed as an omnibus formula or principle of modern

analysis, we could say that the more reduced a thing is the truer it becomes. We ought not to wonder when the Nazis claimed a human life was worth only the cost of a few grams of chemical products, or the Marxists maintained that man was the product of economic indoctrination and hence completely subject to State control and exploitation. These are predictable extremes, for without the transcendent hope that characterized the older vision of man, rationalism drifts preferentially and finally obsessively toward materiality. As Jacques Maritain writes:

"Rationalistic reason ends up intoxicated with matter."[24]

L. AFTER RETRENCHMENT

Probably very little of what I have written in the preceding pages was apparent between 1650 and 1700 when Europe committed itself fully to modernity and began to veer in the direction of what we have been calling "the second theory of mankind." Nevertheless, no longer able to stem what it considered to be a rising heretical tide and horrified by nationalistic and philosophical excesses, Spain stepped back from the emerging new order. In the light of history, the Spanish attitude is as understandable as it is questionable. For we cannot help but wonder what could have happened if instead of turning its back on Europe Spain had stayed on the European stage to voice objections and suggest alternatives. If by arms or theology it could no longer prevail, could it at least have helped persuade modernity to take a more humane and appealing turn?

It is important to keep in mind that the Spanish retrenchment did not mean renunciation of its ancient ideals. So great was the conviction that Spain had been chosen of God to maintain the Catholic unity of Europe that even after that high calling proved to be superior to its material strength it was still the only cause that was compatible with its spirit. As Menéndez Pidal writes: "Even though all hope was lost for its old political aim, Spain preferred to drowse in it without the strength to create new national purposes in keeping with the new times that historical development had brought to Europe."[25]

From our standpoint today it seems clear that for centuries Western man has lived in intimate conflict with himself. For despite his original futuristic, open-ended, and possibly everlasting condition—who has knowledge enough to deny it?—he has heeded most in modern times those who advocate the "second theory" of human life, those who have gone to great lengths to convince him that his life is a brief interlude, "a useless passion," "full of sound and fury signifying nothing." It is a message endlessly repeated—and now infinitely boring—in art, literature, and philosophy under as many rubrics as you please but always with the underlying note of desperation, if not of despair. To borrow one of Eugene O'Neill's titles, life is a "long day's journey into night."

The traditional question has been, where did Spain go wrong? For the consensus that the history of Europe is simply what happened and therefore what should have happened contrasts vividly with the opposing assumption that the history of Spain is what should not have happened. Seen from this perspective, the proper history of Spain would be what did not take place but ought to have happened. Thus, an implicit moral condemnation, nowhere more apparent than among the Spanish themselves, infects the entire history of modern Spain.

Perhaps now in the aftermath of its modern calamities, it is time to ask whether and where Europe erred. Julián Marías poses the question this way: "Is it evident that Europe has been what it was supposed to be, that it had no other possibility than the one that actually came to pass?"[26] Lesslie Newbigin puts it even more suggestively: "It might be...that the history of Western Man in the past two hundred years has been shaped by an illusion. And it might be that the signs, manifest all around us, of the disintegration of this culture of ours are ultimately attributable to that illusion."[27]

If indeed Europe and West have been duped by misleading modern illusions, then it is also likely that the ultimate sources of its unique creativity are not its stylish modern theories and ideologies, but the treasury of faith, enthusiasm, and humanitarian idealism deposited in the Western soul ages ago by the transcendent vision of human life. In any case, in recent times alarming symptoms of disintegration announce the depletion of these spiritual reserves.

Never quite seduced by modernity to begin with, for two centuries Spain lingered indecisively at the fringes of the modern world, alternately fascinated and repelled by its lures. But around 1900 Spanish writers and artists began to sense that modernity had entered into its death throes and that the time had come for Spain to shake off its lethargy and reassess its role and reality in the world. In former ages Spain had discovered much of the known world. Now it was time to rediscover Spain itself.

This brings us to the epoch of 1898.

Chapter 4:
Beyond Modernity the Generations of 1898

A. THE QUEST: THE FIRST GENERATION OF 1898

1900. By all reasonable measures Spain seemed finished. The last remnants of its empire were gone, its political institutions were in shambles, its universities, a disgrace, and its people, frustrated and dispirited. But instead of entering into an age of stagnation, Spain experienced another of its remarkable, almost miraculous, recoveries that from time to time in its long history have lifted it from mediocrity to greatness. It was through the phenomenon I refer to as the "Generations of 1898" that the spirit of Spain manifested itself in a particularly intense way, and it is to this manifestation that we must turn in our quest to describe it.

Elsewhere I have written at some length on the nature of generations.[1] My purpose here is not to repeat those efforts but simply to glean from the several generations in the 1898 series their prodigious contributions to the theme of Spain.

With a margin of imprecision characteristic of genuine human events, the first Generation of 1898 began to make its presence felt sometime around 1900. A good many scholars (Inman Fox, for instance), troubled by this and other uncertainties, have raised doubts about the wisdom of applying the term "generation" to this celebrated grouping. It has become fashionable in recent years to deny that it was ever more than a seductive catchword that persists as a literary convenience even though it names nothing real.

Perhaps the underlying reason for this negative hypothesis can be traced to an error of perspective. We seek in vain, as critics of that period have sought, for harmonies and like-mindedness among the leaders of these generations. Instead, their bonds are more often than not polemical even in cases where cordiality and friendships may prevail. Yet rather than disproving their generations, this very dissonance turns out to be our best proof of generational reality. For it points the way to the common themes around which these intellectuals clustered and about which they were as often in passionate disagreement. This is why instead of dwelling on abundant individual idiosyncrasies and singularities, I shall try to construct a more elusive "biography of generational likeness," as Laín Entralgo puts it, always bearing in mind the polemical nature of this collective "likeness."

I begin with what others have noted. There seems to be no question that in or around 1900 the first signs of a new artistic and intellectual sensitivity became evident in Spain. Near the end of the nineteenth century and the beginning of the twentieth Spaniards began to speak of "our time" from a new perspective and with a different intensity. Without being precise where precision is not possible, around this date we find a watershed that divides two centuries and two ways of understanding Spain.

The first symptoms of the new sensitivity appear early in the century in the writings of Azorín, Pío Baroja, Miguel de Unamuno, and Gabriel Maura, among others. But it is important to point out that these new tendencies had to contend with opposing opinions. Their subsequent celebrity does not hide the fact that in its early years this group of intellectuals was viewed with more annoyance than respect. Julio Cejador, for instance, denounced this so-called "generation" as merely a group of young writers led astray by the <u>Institución de Libre Enseñanza</u>. Since the Spanish defeat in 1898 he writes that they "...had conceived in their hearts a mortal hatred for the Spanish tradition and Christian spirit that informed it, engrossing themselves instead in reading the bitter enemy of the Gospel, Friedrich Nietzsche. The loss of the Colonies, which they called the Disaster, a poor rendering of the French *débâcle*, seemed to them, in keeping with the doctrines that were boiling in their heads and the feelings they caressed in their hearts, to be the full confirmation of their positions and the necessary consequence of the spirit and way of being of old Spain."[2]

In Cejador's vitriolic dismissal of these young writers we see the limited initial impact made by this generation. Furthermore, from the outset some of its most illustrious "members"—Baroja, for example, and later Valle-Inclán—either doubted the existence of such a grouping or else denied that it had anything to do with them.

Baroja's testy attitude toward his generation parallels a similar view among his peers regarding the Restoration era (1874-1898). We find harsh condemnations of that period in the earlier writings of these young intellectuals. Indeed, very likely the generalized negative image of the Restoration, which included some of the most brilliant Spaniards of modem times— Galdós, Clarin, Pardo Bazán, Valera, Canovas, Castelar, Sagasta, Menéndez y Pelayo, Ramón y Cajal, among others—is a lingering result of these youthful outbursts.

We need to keep in mind another factor of considerable weight in the fin de siècle period: the seductive image of the literary and intellectual *enfant terrible*. Oscar Wilde and Nietzsche come to mind. By this time the old Voltairian satire on traditional beliefs and philosophical absurdities was evolving into the rhetorical strategy of shock—*épater le bourgeois*—for its own sake. And there was more to come: what began as a zestful tweaking of the old rules of decorum and beauty became in the course of the twentieth century a hostility to classic aesthetic and moral canons. The cult of ugliness had begun.

By the end of the nineteenth century and the beginning of the twentieth in Europe, just as religious faith was more and more restricted to remote corners of life away from meaningful public affairs, so art found itself being reduced to little more than a curiosity and an amusement. Whereas once it claimed to speak earnestly from center stage to all mankind and assumed nothing less than responsibility for the human condition itself, now those prerogatives had passed by default into the hands of scientists and politicians. Because they were no longer taken seriously, artists and writers were ceasing to be serious. Stripped of social responsibility, they were beginning to act irresponsibly.

But if some members of the first generation of 1898 were tempted by the image I have just described, the Spanish public was hardly ready to tolerate such self-indulgent frivolity. It still required responsible art and ideas from its creative minds, especially those of a philosophical or theoretical bent. The real or presumed weakness of their public and political institutions caused Spaniards to take seriously what their creative artists and writers had to tell them. They could hardly afford frivolity for its own sake. Unlike their European and American counterparts, who at the time were being pushed from the center stage of public life by the new and more aggressive sciences of statecraft and nature, the Spanish intellectuals and artists of 1898 were assuming nothing less than the destiny of Spain itself.

Consequently, this cluster of young writers and artists came of age in a cultural milieu modulated by a new sense of patriotic and intellectual responsibility. Probably for that reason they often wrote with a caustic severity beyond their years. We hear it, for instance, in these words of Joaquín Costa: "...Since the death of Cisneros the Spanish State has lived in a perpetual Sunday," and in Ortega's early pronouncement: "The Restoration...was a panorama of phantasms, and Cánovas was the great impresario of the phantasmagoria." Recalling those early years and Spain's bleak prospects, Antonio Machado writes these gloomy verses:

> *Fue ayer; éramos casi adolescentes; era*
> *Con tiempo malo, en cinta de lúgubres presagios,*
> *(It was yesterday, we were hardly more than*
> *adolescents; the times were ominous, pregnant with*
> *dark forebodings)*

Or again:

> *Castilla miserable, ayer dominadora,*
> *Envuelta en sus andrajos. desprecia cuanto ignora.*
> *(Wretched Castile, yesterday dominant,*
> *Wrapped in her rags, she despises all she does not*
> *know.)*

But these pessimistic notes occasionally resonate contrapuntally with the hope of a resurrected Spain, as Machado writes:

> *Una España implacable y redentora,*
> *España que alborea.*
> *(An implacable and redemptive Spain,*
> *A Spain that is dawning.)*

These youthful intellectuals who felt burdened—perhaps not without Romantic self-consciousness—by the responsibility for a defeated and humiliated Spain also felt isolated, and at times alienated. For even though they were united by friendships, literary collaborations, and what Luis Granjel has called "an early awareness of...brotherhood," there was little cohesion. Their individual idiosyncrasies made it next to impossible for them to coexist amicably as a spiritual guild or fraternity. Unsure of themselves, perhaps because of their youth and isolation, **they assumed that only by being different could they be themselves at all.** And they resembled one another collectively in their fierce individual determination not to be like anyone else. But we can look on this trait more benignly if we remember that they lived in an age that commonly mistook eccentricity for originality. Hence the extravagant, neo-Romantic *personas* in which some of them cloaked themselves. Later, under the somewhat paradoxical tutelage of Ortega—for it was a case of youth instructing the mature—Azorín and Baroja learned that the intellectual endeavor need not consist of an existential estrangement from ordinary life but instead could be carried out with a certain social normalcy. As for Unamuno, an imposing presence but provincially isolated and hurt after several periods of exile, these lessons went unlearned, or at least unheeded.

But we should bear in mind that if they were isolated from something, that something was Spain itself, which meant, paradoxically, that they were bonded to Spain by their very isolation from it. Theirs was an empty, unsatisfactory relationship expressed as an estrangement, but it was a relationship nonetheless.

We have heard the vituperative tone of their comments about the pretense and shallowness of Restoration Spain. Yet we need to balance these negative views with certain other facts. Far from being the cultural wasteland they often made it out to be, late Restoration Spain offered a repertory of artistic techniques, models, works, and talents that were not only admirable in themselves but also comparable to the best that Europe had to offer.

From their point of view, however, Restoration intellectualism and art were misapplied. It was not that the Restoration writers and intellectuals were insensitive to the problem of Spain. Far from it: writers like Galdós, Pereda, and Pardo Bazán were surely as aware of the "problem" of Spain as their younger contemporaries, and they showed their concern in their works. In fact, these youthful diatribes against the Restoration may be taken as an oblique acknowledgement of the prestige enjoyed by the venerable figures of previous generations. What set the new generations apart was not so much a superiority of talents and patriotism as their more intense anguish and, especially, their unswerving drive to achieve the most radical and rabid authenticity in their art.

If the young writers of 1898 were slow to recognize the merits of Restoration Spain, for a long time they also seemed uncertain of their own importance and showed no great confidence in their contributions. Furthermore, the century was well under way before they gained noticeable social stature. They were not politicians or statesmen and for many years enjoyed only modest fame as writers.

But there is another factor that probably has not received enough attention. Their anguish over Spain was not an exclusive agenda of national problems but an inner, spiritual uneasiness with a tendency to become a kind of far-reaching but carefully disguised inferiority complex. For this reason, the crisis of Spain and the initial skepticism with which this young generation viewed conventional Spanish history and institutions were at the same time and at another level a continual personal crisis. For as they pondered the problematical nature of Spanish reality, they were persuaded that their lives were composed of the same spiritual essence as their nation. And there was no escaping the identification with their land. Their bond to Spain was too profound to turn revolutionary. Consequently, there was never any serious question of rejecting the essence of Spain that was also the substance of their lives. As we saw earlier, they shared the common Spanish trait of believing that their history was what they were and not merely something they possessed. As a result, in those early years the vehemence of their convictions regarding the ills of Spain was matched only by the fervor of their self-doubts. Although they were inalienably committed to Spain, they also doubted it, which meant that at a certain level they also doubted themselves.

But here we need to pause to remind ourselves that this generation—and the ones that followed—was not limited to a handful of egregious intellectuals. The usual list of famous names would include Unamuno, Azorín, the brothers Machado, Antonio and Manuel, Maeztu, Valle-Inclán, Ramón y Cajal, Menéndez Pidal, Baroja, and Ganivet. But these were by no means the only members of that generation. It would be more accurate to say they were representative but not exclusive. They were accompanied in their generational march by uncounted millions of companions.

Although what I call here the "coordinates" of the new generational sensitivity are credited, and rightly so, to the stellar intellectuals of 1898, it remains an open question whether at a deeper level these new spiritual promptings were created outright by the few or distilled by them f om the many into the Spanish *Zeitgeist*. In any case, it seems these intellectual leaders were able to exert what became a remarkable example of spiritual leadership only because the masses responded enthusiastically to their message.

The neo-Romantic tendencies evident in the attitudes and works of the new generation—Valle-Inclán and Manuel Machado, for example—have given rise to many conjectures about their relationship to the older Romantics and Modernists like Rubén Darío. Laín Entralgo offers some of the most balanced views in his classic work La generación de noventa y ocho (The Generation of 1898). But these melodramatic gestures, a preference for grandiose titles for their works, and an undeniable propensity for anguish, which Ortega deplored so much, do not fully explain their aloof indifference to the "realistic" and otherwise splendid works of the Restoration writers. Nor do we fully describe them simply by labeling their own work "Romantic" or "neo—Romantic."

The same could be said for their Modernist traits. (Here we also need to keep in mind our earlier premise that the strains of Romanticism reach far deeper into history than the "Romantic" era itself.) For them the older writers had embraced a realism, which though fully realistic was not fully real. For even though it dealt with real conditions, its techniques were largely imported and not a function of Spanish reality itself.

The unswerving determination of the young writers of 1898 to achieve a "rabid authenticity," to use Marías' term, obligated them to create not only original works but also something more fundamental. I refer to a new generic style within which literary genres evolved that necessitated in turn new metaphors of life and new existential modes.

Here we find one of the keys to understanding the polemical posture they took regarding the Restoration writers. The latter—Galdós, Valera, Clarín, Picón, Pardo Bazán, Pereda, among others—certainly wrote at "the height of the times," as Ortega might have said, but that height was precisely the problem for the younger writers who hungered for a greater spiritual altitude and a superior vision of Spain.

Because they were so keenly attuned to current controversies, the Restoration writers commonly incorporated in their works the socially relevant ideas and intellectual cliches of the day. Think of the masterful way Galdós treated such matters as religious intolerance, class imbalances, and the conflict between the values of old Spain and modern Europe. In other words, they wrote what everybody already knew. Hence the general popularity of their work.

But insofar as these ideas were popular, they were correspondingly less personal. In general, we do not meet Galdós or Pereda on the printed page. They speak with evident sincerity and eloquence for the public, but their message is socially scripted by prevailing expectations. Consequently, we do not experience that intimate awareness of the author who has personally created every line of his work. To use Marías' term, they lack "page quality."

With the new generation we feel a rise in the literary temperature as a shortening of the distances occurs not only between writer and theme but also, and more strikingly, between writer and reader. The circle grows tighter and more intimate, for some readers uncomfortably so. Think of Unamuno who "gets in the face" of his readers.

Having rejected the standard literary fare that consisted of transmuted themes from European bourgeois society modulated either by Comtian positivism or scientific naturalism, the young intellectuals of 1898 found a model more to their liking in the sardonic and pessimistic writings of Mariano José de Larra. It goes without saying that by 1900 Romanticism as a way of life and canonical form of art—always excepting music—had subsided both in Spain and the rest of Europe. The last social vestiges of Spanish Romanticism were swept away by the disturbances of 1868, grandly mislabeled "The Glorious" (*La Gloriosa*). But as Laín Entralgo points out, the most outstanding intellectuals of 1898 were provincials. They were able to discover Castile and Madrid precisely because they were not Castilians or *Madrileños*. They came from peripheral regions and small towns where an antiquated romanticism lived on in customs, music, and, more importantly, mothers and grandmothers.

Even though respectable arguments have been advanced to prove that the neo-Romantic and archaizing tendencies in the writers of 1898 can be traced to these early influences, they fail to account for the most important features of their work and thus must be viewed with some skepticism. Perhaps it would be more accurate to say that the younger writers appealed to their Romantic grandparents for a certain moral justification in their dispute with their Restoration parents. But despite these sympathetic bonds, the "grandsons" of Romanticism had no intention of resurrecting the old Romantic agenda. A portion of their trajectory paralleled Romanticism but it went much farther and ultimately veered in an altogether different direction.

By rejecting the style—literary and social—of the Restoration, the young intellectuals of 1898 left themselves no choice but to make a maximum creative effort. Their radical pact with truth and life demanded it, as did the courageous but paradoxical acceptance of their unacceptable Spanish condition and impossible personal situation. Pérez de Ayala would say a few years later in Prometeo that fin de siècle Spain seemed to his generation to be "...the country of impossibilities."

Thus, the first generation of 1898 annulled the implicit Restoration pact with the genteel codes of a status quo dominated by urbane good taste and elevated rhetorical forms and initiated an intensely personal literature. Instead of writing works already half finished by the prevailing social norms and literary criteria of the day, they committed themselves to creating original works from the most intimate depths of their lives. This is why they ferociously resisted—perhaps to a fault—any societal intrusion into their individual priorities.

Contrary to what has nearly always been presumed, in some cases it was not a question of superior literary gifts. If this was sometimes true, in other instances we are struck by the ironic contrast between the intense genius of these youthful intellectuals and, occasionally, their relatively modest literary gifts. Compared to the graceful literary talents of Galdós, Clarín, Pereda, or Valera, for example, Baroja's novels often seem pedestrian and carelessly crafted. Yet if the Restoration writers were often better at artistically manipulating socially attested commonplaces, the first generation of 1898 rose to a higher order of magnitude in its discovery of new zones and unexplored depths of Spanish reality, especially in the way they personally appropriated these new dimensions and treated them from new perspectives. To summarize these generational differences, it was a question of different levels of radicality. For whereas the older generations were unsurpassed at rendering the commonplace aesthetically appealing, the intellectuals of 1898 launched unprecedented and sometimes inexpert probes into unexplored strata of the Spanish mode of being.

Perhaps this very sensation of sailing blind into uncharted oceans of the Spanish psyche renders more acute the sense of urgency and shipwreck (*naufragio*) we find in their work. Obviously, these feelings were externally exacerbated by the military disaster of 1898, which culminated a century of political drift and a quarter century of political pretense. But within a few years the pain and memory of the "Disaster" faded somewhat from public consciousness, whereas their particular _angst_ persisted, in some cases becoming even more pronounced with maturity.

I may have misnamed their concerns. For if they were occasionally agitated by the sort of existential dread that appears in Kierkegaard and was later elaborated by Heidegger, more often they were moved by what Azorín variously called *ansia de altura* and *idealismo exaltado*, that is, a yearning for a higher plane of art and life. This longing may have begun as an inverse reaction to the style and politics of the Restoration with its grandiloquent rhetoric and sterile parliamentarianism, but it soon evolved into something more positive and promising, even though still tentative.

Feeling the accumulated weight of two centuries of embarrassing Spanish inferiority and aggravated by the debacle of 1898, the new generation proposed the radical solution of overcoming what many took to be the presumptive historical destiny of Spain. Naturally they were not the first to offer remedies for Spain's maladies, but unlike the earliest "regenerationists" such as Joaquín Costa or Macías Picavea who attributed the ills of Spain to inept governments or the "*austricismo*" of the Monarchy, the younger members of 1898 soon came to believe that political adjustments were mere palliatives for the symptoms, not cures for the disease itself. It is true that initially many of the younger intellectuals joined their older contemporaries in calling for a general Europeanization of Spain. But this enthusiasm soon faded and except for Azorín, who continued to insist for a number of years on a socialistic agenda, so did their confidence in political strategies and especially in political parties. Even though Unamuno himself had said in 1895 that "Spain is still to be discovered, and only Europeanized Spaniards can discover it," in later writings he cried out against the harmful effects of an exaggerated Europeanization that he equated with Cartesian rationalism. For he had come to believe—or perhaps always had—that modern reason was in direct conflict with the Christian faith and in such writings as <u>My Religion</u>, <u>The Agony of Christianity</u>, and <u>The Tragic Sense of Life</u> he insisted on the irreducible nature of the Catholic and Quixotic spirit of Spain and its incompatibility with the prestigious but impoverished truths of what he derided as European "Kultura."

This change of attitude brings us to a turning point and to a new phase. For nearly a decade the first generation of 1898 decried the shortcomings of the Restoration, suffered the shock and humiliation of the "Disaster," and was tempted by what we could call the "quick fix" of imitative or imported Europeanism. From then on, however, while not ceasing to be concerned for the immediate political and institutional problems of historical Spain, this first generation turned its attention more and more to intrahistorical Spain. They had inherited a much-troubled country and for several years were nonplussed by the sheer magnitude of its contemporary problems. But gradually as they artistically transcended the perceived sordidness of their condition, they looked beyond the distressed Spain of modern history and began to probe the much greater potentialities of essential Spain.

They searched for this transcendent Spain in its three primary manifestations: the past, the people, and the landscape. Probably no artistic period has ever been more visual in its portrayals. It is important, however, to understand that their vision was not limited to the objective perspectives of the old positivist or the realist, nor to the narcissistic and apostrophic images of the Romantics, nor yet to the transcendent objectivism of the phenomenologists. Every new art arises as a new species of visuality and hence a new relationship with reality. This generation of writers was able to create new styles, including literary styles, because they first learned to see things—and seeing must be learned—in a radically different way.

Our first impression is that they merely portray prosaic things in the simple hierarchies of their natural appearance. Yet as we examine their work more closely, we see that simplicity was not a simple matter at all but the distilled product of a carefully crafted style that coaxes the shy splendor of humble things into revelation by maintaining an exquisite fidelity to their condition. In this Azorín was the unquestioned master. **For they understood that things are prosaic only because we have not loved them and consequently have not elicited their hidden beauties.** Theirs is a style that tends to shun artificial adornment, for the world around them is itself more than enough for their art. This is why in general they avoid the "inexpressive superlatives," as Azorín put it, which had become the standard clichés of modern poetic idiom. We are tempted to compare their general style to Gonzalo de Berceo or the medieval Romances until we realize that far from the guileless naïveté of the European Middle Ages, for the Writers of 1898 simplicity was a hard-won achievement, a difficult triumph over a long tradition of baroque syntax, mythological imagery, and Romantic panegyrics. They determined that even the humblest things had a right to speak for themselves in an idiom consonant with their reality, more, that if allowed to do so, they had unsuspected nuggets of truth and beauty to offer. This generation considered it a moral imperative not to let anything—including language—come between them and the objects of their contemplation.

In summary, this generation conceived a grand love for Spain, a love with a broad register of filial and erotic notes. And as lovers are wont to do, they desired to know everything about their beloved. In the altruistic effusiveness of their passion, they far exceeded the prosaic limits of the realistic style, just as they surpassed the vague sensibilities of the Romantics. Like all lovers, in moments of exultation they turned lyrical, but it was an understated lyricism for theirs was also a sober—and sometimes hard—love that looks on the beloved's faults and is not shaken. Inevitably—as in all true loves—there were moments of heartache. Yet any other destiny would have been unthinkable, for like all true love their passion for Spain was irrevocable.

In some cases, real or fictitious, their pain is greater than their strength and their unbreakable ties to an intolerable reality assume tragic dimensions. In their grief they fall into a spiritual listlessness, into *abulia,* according to a popular expression of the times, which sometimes reached self-destructive extremes.

Ganivet in real life and protagonist Andrés Hurtado of Baroja's El árbol de la ciencia illustrate the point. Of the latter Baroja writes:

> *This lad did not have the strength to live.*
> *He was an Epicurean, an aristocrat, even though he did not think so. But he had something of a precursor in him...*

In most cases, however, this irrevocable love for Spain was able to withstand the painful sordidness that confronted it because it looked beyond these contemporary blights. As they began to explore Spain, they not only discovered its deeper beauties but were also heartened by its human meaning. They found prima facie evidence of Spanish originality and this, despite all the distractions and the ugliness around them, allowed these youth to gain strength and have hope.

In this way the first generation of 1898 removed from Spain its old stigma of monstrosity. With "overwhelming tenderness," in the words of Azorín, this generation undertook the supreme task of reviving Spain. Ortega would say later that they injected blood into the veins of the dead.

All this, conceived in love and spurred on by the unshakable conviction that Spain was infinitely greater than its defective parts and immeasurably superior to its lamentable politics and recent history, stands as permanent achievements of this remarkable generation. But there is more. They had at least one more significant move to make during their generational trajectory. For not only did they reveal the profound reality of Spain, they also took possession of this revelation. In doing so they reached an unexplored dimension of Spanish reality, which was not simply an objective acknowledgement seen from the outside but a virtually unlimited plane that consists in being possessed from within. In this way their art and their intimacy become one. They intuited what Ortega was to convert into a phenomenological method in <u>Meditations on Quixote</u>, which is that reality, always modest and evasive, yields only its external and incidental features to the rational and political contentions of men. Speaking for his generation in <u>Juan de Mairena</u>, Machado argues that true reason, humanized reason, to which the evasive world reveals its most beautiful secrets, is the offspring of an erotic dialogue between intellect and truth. For we truly know only what we truly love.

This noble love engendered other noble sentiments, and through these high ideals of altruistic understanding that flowed from it this generation was able in time to transcend its earlier antipathies toward its own past as well as certain jingoistic tendencies toward Europe. It would stretch the truth to say that these traits disappeared entirely. Unamuno, for example, never abandoned the conviction that European rationalism was the enemy of life and the antithesis of everything that intra-historical Spain had stood for over the ages. From this extreme position He brooked no intellectual rebuttal. Yet on a different level he circumvented his own polemical stand against the hated abstractions of rationalism and science by a personal appeal to his "brothers" of faith and flesh everywhere. What his mind denied, his spirit allowed. The result was that without compromising the uniqueness of their Spanish vision and passion, the first generation of 1898 went on to make a majestic statement on the universal human condition.

But as it reached the plenitude of its vision, the first generation of 1898 also began to reveal its limitations. These creative minds laid out the coordinates of their age by taking amorous possession of Spanish reality, past, present, and possible. They apprehended it in its human integrity from what Baroja called the "unbribable core" of their being. But they did so perhaps without fully understanding what they were collectively about, or if they did without bothering to explain it. For this generation was not always above surrounding their discoveries with a halo of mystery tinged by a note of presumptuousness. In any case, literature alone, even the works of genius produced by this generation, was not enough to complete the Spanish resurrection. But we must admit that it was what Julián Marías calls the "literary temper" of this generation that opened the door to the true restoration of Spain to itself.

The first generation by no means had finished its work at this point. Nevertheless, around 1913-14 what we may call its "first phase" culminates and the second begins. If isolation marked its first period, collaboration—willing or not—was the rule thereafter. Two works in quick succession mark the transition. The first is Unamuno's <u>Del sentimiento trágico de la vida</u> (1913) and the second, Ortega's <u>Meditaciones del Quijote</u> (1914). For the moment I am less interested in the specific content of those works than in their significance as markers of a generational transition.

With this we see emerging what I call the "Second Generation of 1898," by which, to repeat, I mean the second in the historical era that began around 1900.

B. THEORETICAL ORIENTATION: THE SECOND GENERATION.

Manuel Azaña, Pablo Azcárate, Américo Castro, Eugenio d'Ors, Enrique Díez-Cañedo, Manuel García Morente, Salvador de Madariaga, Federico de Onís, José Ortega y Gasset, Pedro

Salinas, Gabriel Miró, Joan Miró, Pérez de Ayala, Eduardo Marquina, Ramiro de Maeztu, Ramón Gómez de la Serna, Julio Rey Pastor, Fernando Vela, Claudio Sánchez Albornoz, Melchor Fernández Almagro, Juan Ramón Jiménez, Gregorio Marañón, Pablo Picasso, and millions of other Spaniards: this is the generation of 1915-16.

The first thing that strikes us in this "second" generation is the numerical increase of the artistic and intellectual minority. This was to have an immediate consequence, for even though its outstanding personalities were comparable in genius to their elders, because of their greater numbers their generational profile is less pronounced. If we add the vague understanding of what generations are to begin with, then we can understand why some used to debate whether Ortega ought to be included in the same generation as Unamuno. But by Ortega's own generational reckoning there can be no doubt that he belongs to the second generation of the series.

At the same time, we must emphasize the "cumulative" character of this generation presided over by Ortega. For if the two generations were not always in agreement, they were in general accord regarding their common endeavor: the rediscovery, resurrection, and historical projection of Spain, its culture and its life.

We have seen how the first generation of 1898, having rejected the Restoration era and its postulates, approached the problems of Spain from an elevated historical and literary perspective, and we have already alluded to the "literary temper" that characterized its work. Yet this effort included the rigorous studies of scholars such as Menéndez Pidal and Asín Palacios, who with their disciples contributed so much to the reconstruction of medieval Spain. In general terms, we can say that thanks to the collective efforts of thinkers, poets, novelists, artists, and scholars of 1898 a much more reasonable historical panorama of Spain emerged. One of their imperishable legacies—for there are several—was removing from Spain its old obscurantist and monstrous labels.

There came a moment, however, when the need for a coherent and rigorous theory of Spain became acute. We have already seen how and for different reasons Unamuno and Ganivet, the most theoretically inclined minds of that era, made only limited efforts to develop a theoretical base for their work. In the case of Unamuno, the lack shows. After <u>The Tragic Sense of Life</u> he could advance no further intellectually along this anti-rational, anti-theoretical road. Literarily, it was a different matter, of course, and for the rest of his life he creatively recycled the ideas of that great work in his novels and poetry.

The second generation with its "philosophical temper," as Marías describes it, came to the rescue of the first. Thus began a rare generational symbiosis that was to have notable consequences, among them an appreciable acceleration in Spanish intellectualism.

It would be a mistake, however, to think that the generation of 1915-16 began its work with intact and mature theories. At first the new generation assumed with even greater fervor the early Europeanizing posture of its predecessor. Thus, the young Ortega said that Spain was the problem and Europe, the solution to it.

At the time probably nothing else could be expected of the younger generation. Unlike their older contemporaries who were to a large degree autodidactic provincials with noticeable xenophobic tendencies, the younger intellectuals and artists were imbued from the start with European cosmopolitanism of the *Belle Époque*. Eugenio d'Ors appeared to be almost as much at home in the cultures and languages of France and Italy as he was in those of his native Barcelona. The personal circumstances of Ortega and Pérez de Ayala, which included residence and study abroad, caused them to establish permanent ties to European intellectuality, especially in Germany, at the time undoubtedly the most prestigious in the world. We should not wonder, then, that because of these experiences Ortega was able to teach Azorín and Baroja, as well as to contemporaries of his own generation—Juan Ramón Jiménez, for instance—lessons on the patterns of European intellectual life. Commenting on this relationship, Torrente Ballester wonders: "How many of their qualities have the men of 1898 been aware of thanks strictly to Ortega?"[3]

The inevitable comparisons made with their own country as a result of this European experience were institutionally unfavorable to Spain. The superiority of foreign universities, laboratories, and intellectual resources in the more materially advanced European countries was beyond question. Yet at the same time Ortega and others became aware that on the personal plane no such superiority was detectable. Indeed, the contrary was more often true and the paradoxical reasons for it evident. Lacking solid intellectual and scientific traditions, Spanish intellectuals had no other alternative but to seek knowledge beyond the boundaries of Spain. This meant that a command of other languages and a comprehensive knowledge of different modes of thinking and other ways of life were indispensable first steps, for they had no choice but to be open to the main European intellectual and scientific channels.

To their surprise and astonishment these young Spanish students discovered that the same was not true of many European intellectuals. Separately convinced of their own superiority, Germans and Frenchmen often were unaware of, and unconcerned, with what was happening in the neighboring country. And much the same could be said for the English. They were afflicted with the reverse provincialism of those who reside in the great centers of the world and smugly assume that nothing worthy can happen beyond its boundaries.

In The Tragic Sense of Life Unamuno asked, is truth to be lived or to be understood? He presented the supposed antithetical relationship of pure reason and life (already suggested in Kierkegaard's Either/Or, which Unamuno admired so much), the leitmotiv of that great work, as the burdensome conflict of modern mankind.

Ortega was not long in responding, pointing out in Meditations on Quixote that truth is to be understood by living, for life in the Ortegan sense is reason in action, while the abstract reason against which Unamuno railed was only a limited dimension of the all-inclusive "vital reason" (which also could be called "historical" and "narrative" reason.) "Pure reason," writes Ortega, "cannot supplant life: When confronted with spontaneous culture the culture of the abstract intellect is not another sort of self-sufficient life, nor can it dislodge life. It is only a small island floating in the sea of primal vitality."[4]

Although as far as we know Ortega made no explicit references to The Tragic Sense of Life, his indirect hints—including commentaries in his correspondence—allow us to suppose that Unamuno's passionate and persuasive work alarmed him, since it was capable of directing Spanish intellectuality toward a philosophical blind alley.[5]

Along with many of his contemporaries who were troubled not only by the extravagant propositions put forth by Unamuno but also by the general lack of theoretical rigor in the older generation, Ortega felt by mid-decade that it was time to begin solidifying his own views. Ever more disenchanted with Unamuno and dissatisfied with the neo-Kantian basis of his own philosophy, Ortega was finally convinced that he had no other choice but to wrest the ideas of life and reason away from the irrationalists and the proponents of Nietzschean Lebensphilosophie and replace them with superior concepts.

For a brief time in 1911-12 Husserlian phenomenology seemed to be the answer for Ortega's generation, for it held out the dual promise of resolving the crisis of reason and transcending the inadequate postulates of neo-Kantianism and positivism. In a posthumous work, Prólogo para alemanes (Prologue for Germans), written in 1934 but unpublished until 1958, Ortega recalls the euphoria of his youthful encounter with phenomenology: "For us phenomenology was not a philosophy: it was...a stroke of good fortune."[6]

This initial impression soon faded and even though phenomenology left its indelible mark on this generation of thinkers, it made few, if any, lasting converts. In another posthumous work La idea de principio en Leibniz y la evolución de la teoría deductiva (The Idea of Principle in Leibniz and the Evolution of Deductive Theory [1958]) Ortega confessed that he"...abandoned phenomenology at the very moment of receiving it."

There were obvious reasons for their early disillusionment. The younger poets and intellectuals of 1915-16 sought to purge their style of the pessimistic sentimentality and emotional personal intrusiveness of their older contemporaries. They preferred a more serenely intellectual and "European" perspective from which to ponder Spain and its problems. Initially the intellectual rigor of phenomenology seemed to suit these purposes. But the deficiencies of Husserlian phenomenology were too glaring to retain their loyalty.

Faithful to his Cartesian roots, Husserl assumed as primary not the evidence of things themselves but an "awareness of' them, and from this curious assumption he proceeded methodologically to "suspend" or reduce for subsequent consideration certain portions of reality, especially the troublesome, spontaneous phenomena of human life.

But Spanish thought since Unamuno and Ganivet—and strictly speaking, at least as early as Gracián—had been moving in the opposite direction. Upon his return from Germany, Ortega proceeded to formalize what was already in the air, namely, that the primary reality is not the Cartesian/Husserlian "awareness of' things and persons, but these very things and persons themselves in all their concrete presence.

Fleeing the tyranny of Cartesian rationalism, the first generation of 1898 allied itself with the irrational, not realizing perhaps that in the name of liberty it was but shackling itself with heavier chains. As the second generation understood things, it was not enough merely to decry with impassioned bluster the problematical foundations of modern thought. For this would mean it was parasitically dependent on the very errors it opposed. Instead, this generation strove to impart a new conceptual rigor to thought—Ortega, d'Ors, Marañón—, and in poetry and the novel—Juan Ramón Jiménez, Ramón Pérez de

Ayala, Gabriel Miró—in order to reach a rarified aesthetic plane compatible with the intellect but averse to both plebeian emotionalism and stylistic pomposity.

Even though both generations perceived the limitations of the abstract reason on which modern philosophy and science rested, on a theoretical level they reacted in very different ways. The first generation opposed it with refractory obstinacy. The second, repulsed by the luddite mentality of their elders, methodically sought to justify it by inserting it into a more comprehensive reason that corresponded to the phenomenologically evident and urgent condition of human life, that is, life in **this** real world which for them was Spain. These efforts culminated in diverse ways: the comparative and restorative historicity popularized by Madariaga and Américo Castro, the medically oriented essays of Marañón, and bringing them all into focus under a common patent, Ortega's celebrated *cogito*: "I am I and my circumstance."

Although it was profoundly innovative, perhaps for that very reason the first generation of 1898 was not especially precocious and, as we have seen, its prestige was late in coming. Pérez de Ayala and Juan Ramón Jiménez achieved fame almost simultaneously with Azorín, Baroja, Valle-Inclán, and the Machado brothers. Because he was older, Unamuno was already well known. Yet even though he boasted of the impact he and his generation had on the youngsters of 1915-16, referring to them as their "sons" or "grandsons," the truth was, as Torrente Ballester noted long ago, "The second generation was born into historical and literary life at a time when the men of 98 were not yet in a position to father anybody. In its cultural instruction, which is one of its determining traits, it owes nothing to the men of 98 whose influence at the time was almost nil."[7]

Unlike its predecessor, the generation of 1915-16 began to display its genius relatively early. This unusual coincidence, the simultaneous rise of two highly endowed generations both dedicated to the rescue and revival of Spanish culture, resulted in a renewal of intellectual and artistic life that was not merely an acceleration along an established axis but a geometrical intensification of a higher order of magnitude. Working together they were able to overcome within a surprisingly few decades the onerous cultural backwardness of Spain, which for centuries had been the cause of national anguish and self-reproach. If Restoration Spain of 1890 was perceived as a laggard in the culture race in Europe, the revitalized Spain of 1930 was, incredible as it may seem, already beginning to take the lead in philosophy, still the most intellectual of disciplines at that time.

This rapid historical transformation did not come about without frictions and in some cases, startling deviations from the mainstream. Maeztu, for example, who began as a fervent anti-traditionalist and advocate of Europeanization, in the end became convinced that the greatness and salvation of Spain lay in being true to its ancient values. As for Unamuno, unused to sharing the limelight, the "congestion" created by the arrival of the new generation seemed to make him uncomfortable. Once benignly avuncular toward his younger contemporaries, later he called them "simpletons" (*papatas*).

We must not overlook another factor. Spain remained neutral during World War I. But this official neutrality does not explain the complex reaction it provoked. Before the eyes of the Spanish intellectuals Europe of the *Belle Époque* in which they had placed their hope and faith and in whose culture they were saturated, was destroying itself in the bloodiest war in history.

Their disappointment could not have been more profound. Spain turned its eyes to Europe just when Europe was turning on itself. How could they hope, therefore, to find solutions to Spain's problems in the midst of such barbarity? Of course this perplexity was not limited to Spanish intellectuals. It also affected their British, French, and German contemporaries whose production between 1918 and 1930 reeks of a pervasive desolation. Conditions in Europe were also a major factor in the first great wave of American pessimism in the famous "Lost Generation" of Ernest Hemmingway, Gertrude Stein, F. Scott Fitzgerald, and others who either took up permanent residence in Paris—Julien Green, for instance—or spent years in voluntary exile in Europe. (In passing, we should note that this "contrived" pessimism was a far cry from the real exuberance and high degree of happiness of American life during that era. It would be fascinating to study how the arts have moved progressively further away from the real stream of life in recent centuries and the degree to which these "fictions" have falsified our views of reality.) It was not only a matter of actual warfare among the great powers but also jingoistic indifference to the kindred cultures of enemy nations. For the first time in modern history, hardly any country admired any other. The old intellectual network in the West, cordial, open, and international since the Enlightenment, was permeated by virulent propaganda, chauvinistic forms of patriotism, or, going to the other extreme, utopian one-world visions. It became fashionable to hate one's neighbors while adoring humanity.

Although Spain was not militarily involved in the war, the climate of discord characteristic of the propaganda broadcast by the belligerents revived old Spanish partisan divisions and within a few years undermined the tacit social concordat that had remained more or less intact since the Restoration. The propagandistic phenomenon—as historically novel as it is generally unnoticed by historians—quickly replaced genuine rhetoric and become one of the most virulent intellectual and political plagues of the twentieth century. Propaganda not only falsified the truth but also eroded the real or feigned homage to truth that had always been the governing ethical assumption of Western life. For the first time, lying shed its hypocritical attachment to truth and justifying itself variously as crass expediency and high ideal, openly proclaimed its right to exist as such. We have only to recall Hitler's "Big Lie," the cynical manipulations of reality by the Marxists, and, not least, the disturbing tendency of the democracies to emulate them, to be aware of the calamitous erosion of truth in recent times.

Falsified by this malignant propaganda, the various brands of European and Western patriotism tended more and more to degenerate into mere jingoism. In the name of the "fatherland" Westerners began to flout the truth openly and to see it not as the authentic ideal of the people but as an obstacle to their crassest political ambitions. Probably it would be an exaggeration, yet with a kernel of truth, to say that it was this sort of propaganda that created the conditions of hatred and distrust that culminated in the Spanish Civil War. When seen from this perspective, the Civil War was the last campaign of World War I and the opening salvos of World War II.

All this was to have extraordinary repercussions in the second generation of 1898. If at first the problems they confronted were seen as purely Spanish to which Europe was their proposed solution, following the atrocities of World War l they realized that this imitative and subordinate posture in regard to Europe would no longer do. Unamuno pointed out in <u>The Agony of Christianity</u> that though colored by different versions of nationalism, the crisis of faith was a modern dilemma that affected all European countries. As for Spain, it was no longer a matter of simply importing science and philosophy. Whether or not other Europeans knew it, Spain might yet prove to be, as Ortega suggested, a "fountain of youth" for old, tired Europe.[8]

Without abandoning in any way, the internal problems of Spain, during the decade 1920-30 the second generation of 1898 began to treat them within a broader context. Rubén Darío and the Modernist school had done much to create interest in Spanish America and to revive on a literary level at least the old Hispanic brotherhood of <u>las Españas</u>. The isolation that had afflicted them on both Atlantic shores was at least partially overcome as art and ideas started to travel in both directions.

Meanwhile, intellectuals like Ortega and Madariaga were beginning to think of Spain not as a poor and needy relative but as an enriching dimension of a Europe in distress and decline. They were starting to conceive of a Spanish Europeanism, a cultural modality that had ceased to exist centuries ago. In some ways, it was the most profound innovation of the era in question and for that very reason yet to be understood in its many implications.

Here, incidentally, we find the final resolution of the old argument between the "Hispanizers" and "Europeanizers." As we look again at this old polemic from the perspective provided by the second generation of 1898, we see that the future of Spain lay in neither camp. Instead, it was up to Spaniards to become who they really always had been: European Spaniards, or better perhaps, Spanish Europeans.

In earlier times Spaniards had reacted, often admirably, to the European cultural imprimatur. But it was due primarily to the work of the second generation that Spaniards ceased to be admiring spectators and began to take an active role in European culture, and more importantly, at the highest levels of that culture. In this sense we can say that works like Ortega's <u>The Revolt of the Masses</u> and <u>The Agony of Christianity</u> of Unamuno were conceived from the standpoint of this "Spanish Europeanism." Hence the extraordinary reception of Ortega's celebrated work. For in this book other Europeans heard a vibrant new voice and an unprecedented message that for all its strange notes they recognized as belonging to the same species of European intellectuality. In other words, both were new but recognizably European. At the risk of simplifying what really happened, from our perspective, we can say that this Spanish Europeanism forged by the first and second generations of 1898 had as its guiding principle the ideal of restoring Spain to itself by vindicating its historic European destiny.

The universalizing tendencies of the second generation affected the first in a climate of concord and in a "cumulative" if not always cooperative spirit. It is another example of a historical phenomenon rarely studied but often repeated—and in our time more than ever—of the influence of the young on the old. Following the example of the younger intellectuals, between 1920 and 1930 the first generation of 1898 tended to moderate its xenophobic proclivities and to assume a more universal and tolerant stance. The happy result was that the older generation had time to alter its course and veer more in harmony with itself, that is to say, with its destiny.

C. ARTISTIC ASSIMILATION: THE THIRD GENERATION

Continuing our generational narrative of the cycle of 1898, we find that the third generation of the that era, those who began to make their historical presence felt about 1930, acted according to patterns established by the preceding generations. What had been an ideal and an aim for the first generations of the series was now a consolidated reality for the third. In the words of Marías, this generation was the first to have "...Spanish teachers in a double sense: creative university professors in possession of fully current methods and valid literary models without archaic features toward which it did not feel any attitude of discord or rupture."[9]

Due to the efforts and achievements of their elders, the way was clear for the intellectual leaders of the third generation. The social profile and public esteem for the intellectual endeavor were now firmly established according to fully assimilated European norms. This was more crucial than it may seem. Instead of having to create for themselves an image and an authentic style, as was the case of the preceding generations, the artists, writers, and thinkers of the third generation could count on a repertory of models and styles unimaginable a few decades earlier.

But after two generations of prodigious creativity, with the advent of the third generation, there occurs a certain change of pace and what appears to be a pause in the theoretical advance. Yet more than a simple rest it turns out to be a moment of artistic assimilation and to a certain degree radicalization of an already vast heritage. Unlike its predecessors who were united—at times polemically—by the same set of problems, the third generation shows a tendency to strike out along unexplored and tangential pathways. Zambrano in thought, Lorca in poetry and theatre, and Dalí in art come to mind.

On the other hand, the artistic and material circumstances of this generation were generally more comfortable than those of their elders. Yet in certain respects this did not work to their advantage. Perhaps the strongest first impression we have of this generation is that it lacks the driving thematic intensity that had been so characteristic of the earlier years of the 1898 era.

Because they were comparatively at ease as the spiritual offspring of the preceding generations, these intellectuals, writers, and artists felt less compelled to venture beyond their comfort zones, and their ambitions shrank accordingly. If Unamuno and Ortega strode with giant steps across their respective generations, the outstanding figures of the third generation projected a more modest image. Xavier Zubiri, for instance, a disciple and later colleague of Ortega, shuddered at the latter's enthusiasm for El Escorial and made clear his—and his generation's—preference for proportions of lesser magnitude.

In addition to the names already cited and always bearing in mind the millions of unsung persons who make up human generations, any list of its celebrated leaders would include Rafael Alberti, Vicente Aleixandre, Dámaso Alonso, Luis Buñuel, Alejandro Casona, Gerardo Diego, Federico García Lorca, Rof Carballo, Laín Entralgo, José Gaos, Lafuente Ferrari, José María Pemán, and Juan Antonio Zunzunegui. Heliodoro Carpintero writes of them: "The aims of their predecessors...were radicalized...The new men would bring to politics the same attitude they had toward science or art...Pure reason in science and politics, and I would almost dare say rational and irrational purity in poetry." [10] At the same time, without being any less literary than their predecessors, they excelled in other artistic genres such as music and the cinema.

The intellectual elite of this generation was conflicted by opposing urges. Many of them proved to be more susceptible than their elders to the mass-centered ideological propaganda that was saturating intellectual life everywhere. Yet on the other hand, they were equally drawn to elitist art. Torrente Ballester said of them: "...this generation begins by proclaiming itself to be a minority: from the beginning it admits the existence of popular art forms, which it rejects as crass and unworthy." [11] Yet this rejection did not always mean abandonment. Think of García Lorca. It would be more accurate to say that they took the raw materials of popular life and transmuted them into poetic gold by enhancing them with new metaphors and a gamut of primary components ranging from classical mythology to contemporary psychoanalytical themes derived from Freud and the Surrealists.

The severest critics of this literature claim to see in the anti-sentimental attitude of its poets, questionable connections with the celebrated "dehumanization of art" popularized by Ortega and practiced to a certain degree by Juan Ramón Jiménez in his later poetry. Ortega was roundly criticized for his notion that poetry could be described as a sort of "algebra" of feelings. Yet neither Ortega nor these elitist poets, who were fascinated for a time by his theories, discard feeling as such. They only questioned whether it was the proper grounding for aesthetics, particularly its more anguished manifestations which they feared all too often degenerated into shallow emotionalism.

All this was a far cry from the circumstances of the first generation of 1898, which saw itself awash in a sea of artistic and cultural mediocrity. The third generation began its work perched solidly on the backs of giants. If mediocrity was the political norm though not the artistic rule of the Restoration, genius had become the standard of the new era. Thus, if the first impulse of the creators of 1898 was to surpass something unacceptable, the initial movement of the third generation was to accept something admirable.

This circumstance conferred on them enormous advantages, but also certain paradoxical disadvantages. In order not to be inferior to their predecessors, the generation of 1930-31 faced the daunting task of assimilating a vast repertory of techniques, themes, styles, and philosophies. Perhaps it was this very zeal for assimilation that created in this generation a tendency toward an elitist remoteness from the public.

Even though restoring Spain to itself remained the most serious and sublime aim of all the generations of 1898, this did not necessarily mean to the generation of 1930-31 that things must always be taken seriously. As a decisive step in his break with the melodramatic art and ideologies of the nineteenth century, Ortega had proclaimed the intranscendent nature of modern art. Art, he argued, could be saved as art only by liberating it from the need to save the world. The younger generation took this message very much to heart, but in its own way. The humorous caricatures of Salvador Dalí and the cinematographic satires of Buñuel on life as the nineteenth century had understood it were prototypical of the new art and in some measure the credo of the new generation.

The aloofness from the public domain was partially offset in this generation by its affinity for an intense private life, especially insofar as friendships were concerned. This was especially true of many of its poets, perhaps its most outstanding figures, who notwithstanding partisan antagonisms caused by the Civil War, continued to be personally loyal to one another. Neither politics nor ideology could break these bonds. Alberti's conversion to proletarian Marxism, for instance, did not affect his personal bond with his fellow poets. Nor, we should add in passing, did it diminish public perplexity over the work he produced after his conversion. He was as misunderstood as a proletarian spokesman as he had been as an elitist poet.

The case of Alberti illustrates to a degree another trait of this generation. Even though its intellectual and artistic leaders became public figures very early, the public was not their foremost concern. They appeared to write preferentially for one another and seemed to delight in caricaturing behind the public's back, as it were, the realisms appreciated by the masses. No wonder they excelled in poetry and painting, the artistic genres that most lend themselves to experimentation and snobbishness.

Perhaps because it came of age at a time when the world was rife with genius and replete with the technical innovations of its predecessors, it seemed relatively easy for this generation to change everything within reach into artistic gold. If its writers could not presume to match the impact of an Ortega or an Unamuno, they handily surpassed the pedestrian style of a Baroja and the early timidities of an Azorín. From the first they were elegantly at ease with their art. Perhaps not without some nostalgic regret and with an oblique reference to his own situation a generation later Marías writes: "This generation, compared to the others of our time, displays a command of facilities over difficulties... the Fairy Godmothers have made a practice of faithfully accompanying the team from the generation of 1901." (1931) [12]

Beyond Modernity the Generations of 1898   149

The third generation seems to be the least committed to the endeavor of resurrecting Spain. Not only the heir to a rich legacy but perhaps the most talented, this generation seems a bit narcissistic. It appeared to pause before the sheer abundance of possibilities. There were so man tempting pathways and so many talents that it hesitated t commit itself irrevocably to any of them. Hence the tendency of its artists and writers to delay permanent commitments and the habit of sampling all the options before them.

On the other hand, this same generation was to experience the violent pressures of propaganda. The old nineteenth-century ideologies had been transmitted principally through bulletins, books, and university circles Moreover, their ideas were comfortably abstract, almost purely "intellectual"—darwinism, socialism, and psychological, scientific, and economic determinism—that hardly affected the daily course of life. Although the content of these doctrines barely changed from one century to the other, the advent of electronic media and mass communication caused the old dogmas, now empowered by new media, to penetrate even the most intimate strata of personal life and to increase their impact exponentially.

At the same time, and partly as a result of what have just described, another largely unnoticed factor came into play. I am referring to certain fundamental difference between the new forms of mass propagandistic suasion and the personal persuasion based on the criteria of classical o traditional rhetoric, which not by coincidence began to disappear from public life during this era. If we are moved by "lyric reasons," as Ortega called them, or convinced by rigorous reasoning, then naturally we respond in these same modes when challenged to explain or justify our position. But if falsehood—the usual traveling companion of hate—binds us to an idea, then infallibly we resort to similar lies in our defense and justification. The tenor of our *explicatio* reveals our real premises.

All these propagandistic phenomena converge with a derogatory view of humanity, what I called in the previous chapter "the second theory of human life." Throughout the twentieth century, but with evident precedents in earlier times, there was an increasing insistence on the primitive, animal nature of mankind. Going a step—or several—beyond the notion of the "human beast" popularized by nineteenth-century psychologists, naturalistic novelists, and scientific Darwinists, their ideological descendants in our time monotonously insist on the dark side of humanity: its predatory and destructive traits.

To these unappealing adjectives we must add another with moral and ethical overtones: despicable. Some time ago certain scientific and intellectual circles stopped admiring the human species. Instead, they look on man as a renegade of nature fit only to pillage and destroy the nurturing world about him. Hence the tacit hostility toward everything that sets man personally apart from nature and the corresponding eagerness to reduce and restrict his kind to a natural phylum. Very likely this same hostility also explains the curious—I was about to say morbid—scientific preference for the most backward and lamentable human cultures. Only wonderfully skewed priorities could cause us to admire wretches who by their own timeless ineptitude are condemned to a short and brutal life of disease, hunger, rain, mud, snakes, flies, and superstitious terrors.

According to this inverted, propagandistic view of human life, far from "lyric reasons" and civil principles, human conduct arises from non-human or infra-human motives. Self-serving and self-centered, man acts cruelly with the gratuitous, unconscious cruelty of an animal. Conscience is but a thin social veneer, and moral conduct altruistic gestures, refined tastes, and respect, mere superficial addenda without real consistency. It is a paradoxical view of human life in which the maximum man is precisely the most minimally human.[13]

The propagandistic media that assumed such potent capabilities during the historical life of the third generation under discussion presuppose this minimalist and manipulative view of mankind. No wonder they were ideally suited and thus soon wed to the rough-hewn ideologies of fascism and Marxism, though we must add that contemporary democracy is not exempt from the same contamination This combination of propagandistic media and ideology has done much to make possible the great totalitarian systems of such sad history in our time. We are emerging from a century that fought mightily over whether man would retain the unique dignity of supernatural personhood or be demoted to a mere means in a totalitarian world and a puny minion in Nature's order.

In view of all this, the elitist tendencies and superior gifts of the third generation of 1898 must be balanced with the false ideological glamour made even more seductive by the Civil War and World War II. Despite its undeniable gifts, there is a tentative, schizophrenic air about this generation, for the sometimes precious intranscendence of its art does not mesh smoothly with the dogmatic zeal of the great ideologies to which some of its members rendered homage. For this reason, it is not surprising—even though regrettable—that some of its most gifted members were swept off their feet, temporarily or permanently, by the propagandistic storms of that era.

In order to be fair our judgment must seem harsh, for to the degree that this and adjacent generations in the West succumbed, they helped establish a norm whereby mere political ideology was allowed to infiltrate and contaminate art. It would prove to be a virulent infection, one from which twentieth-century art and letters never really recovered.

D. CONSOLIDATION: THE FOURTH GENERATION

Outstanding members of the generation that began to make their presence felt in the I 940's include Julián Marías, Camilo José Cela, Miguel Hernández, Dionisio Ridruejo, Luis Rosales, José Ferrater Mora, Enrique Tierno Galván, Gonzalo Torrente Ballester, Germán Bléiberg, Blas de Otero, Carmen Laforet, José María Gironella, Elena Quiroga, Antonio Buero Vallejo, Víctor Ruiz Iriate, and Miguel Delibes. What I have said about the preceding generations is implied in these commentaries and will allow us to abbreviate some of its underlying assumptions and conditions.

In comparison with the third generation, which followed a course that we have described as both tangential and consolidating, the artistic and intellectual leadership of fourth generation is numerically a smaller grouping. And not only numerically reduced but with fewer though more drastic options.

To begin with, the artistic sensitivities developed by the older generations were now irrevocably established and in a certain sense, already classic. The illustrious names, works, and themes of 1898 as well as the enthusiastic reception and response by millions of Spanish and Hispanic followers were consecrated components of a resplendent cultural patrimony. But the historical distance separating the fourth generation from its predecessors was enough for these youthful artists and intellectuals to contemplate their circumstances with a certain detachment. They seemed to have but two fundamental options: either to reaffirm as its guardians what they had inherited or to abandon it.

If the third generation of this series was the most withdrawn, the fourth was the most traumatized by the Civil War and World War II. We need to keep in mind that not only were the latter in their formative years during the Civil War but also that they began their careers amid the oppressive conditions of a dictatorship in its earliest and harshest phase. For this reason, far from being an inherited theme, the venerable "problem of Spain" took on a personal urgency that dispelled any trace of a purely bookish or abstract task.

The intellectual leaders of the fourth generation, who contemplated their past with a certain detachment brought about by skewed circumstances, tended to situate this fidelity or desertion on a personal plane. In many cases within and without Spain theirs was a double isolation. Separated from their teachers and consigned to a marginal status as exiles outside of Spain or subject to severe political repression within their country, they had no other recourse but to grapple alone and unaided with the themes of their art or thought. Probably to a greater degree than the third generation, they were the objects of intense ideological influences. The same propagandistic media that served totalitarian ideologies competed with genuinely Spanish ideas, style, and rhetoric, and unlike Antonio Machado, not all paused "to distinguish the true voices from the false echoes." Hence the frequent "conversions," reaffirmations, transitions, and inflexions that characterized this generation. Think, for instance, of Julián Marías's repeated proclamations of loyalty to the legacy of 1898 and especially to Ortegan thought, Ferrater Mora's conversion to Anglo-American thought, and Tierno Galván's infatuation with Marxism.

Many, perhaps the majority, of those who would later be the intellectual leaders of this generation were in their formative university years when the Civil War broke out. They were eyewitnesses of the intellectual dismantling of institutions, especially the universities, and were forced to make decisions at an early age that would determine the course of their life forever. Many like Maravall pledged their life and fate to preserving the legacy of 1898. Others elected to impose or defend political systems alien to that tradition. But nearly all saw their lives and their ambitions drastically altered. Carpintero describes their dilemma: "...for them, even more than for those of the preceding generation, the war was to be an unavoidable reality that would affect the very root of their lives and would facilitate or menace their future"(Cinco aventuras, p. 21).

As for those who remained faithful to the tradition of 1898 and loyal to the historical roots that sustained it, their solidarity with the past was impervious to temptations and ideological pressures. We should not wonder, then, that at first they began to assume a defensive attitude, at certain moments almost a siege mentality, toward the ominous totalitarianisms of the time. Speaking for himself and his generation, Marías remarks: "We have felt that the future life of Spain was at stake and with it the salvation of all that to us seemed worthy, admirable, original, and irreplaceable in a millennium of Spanish life, and in half a millennium of trans-Spanish, universal creativity."[14]

Even though only a few decades had passed since the beginning of the 1898 era, the intellectual and artistic distance could better be measured in centuries. For during that astonishingly brief historical interval Spain rose from what fin de siecle writers called *marasmo*, or stagnation, and within a few years experienced and cultural renaissance the likes of which Europe and the West had not witnessed in centuries.

Notwithstanding this unparalleled brilliance, the fourth generation of 1898 confronted the critical consensus that because this cultural flowering was politically improbable, it must therefore be impossible, or if not completely so, then at least marginal and limited. It was commonly decreed to have ended ingloriously between 1936 and 1939, thus aborting what came to be called in critical circles of that time, half a golden century.

Yet despite the early reports of its demise, the intellectual leaders of fourth generation, as well as many of its predecessors, survived the Civil War, outlasted the dictatorship, and gave the lie—though not without casualties—to the political and totalitarian falsehoods that will no doubt prove to be embarrassments in a future age when a balanced history of the twentieth century is written.

Even as obituaries were being written for Spanish intellectual life, an impressive array of writers was recharging the Spanish renaissance. Between 1940 and 1950, during the most repressive phase of the dictatorship, Cela, Sastre, Marías, Delibes, Laforet, Romero, Gironella, Matute, and Hierro were beginning their literary careers, while others, and among them Ortega, were reprising theirs. Gómez de la Serna, Zunzunegui, Chacel, Baroja, Azorín, Laín, Menéndez Pidal, and others continued to work uninterruptedly. Nor can we ignore the contributions of the exile community made up of members of this and older generations: among others, Alberti, Jiménez, Castro, Madariaga, Gaos, Zambrano, Pérez de Ayala, Salinas, Ferreter, Guillén, and Sender.

This list of eminent exiles, incomplete to be sure, reminds us once again of the incalculable human and material losses due to the Civil War. Yet not even that calamitous upheaval can obscure the fact that beyond it, or perhaps beneath it, the prevailing generational patterns of Spanish life, though weakened in certain ways and with significant losses in its ranks, continued essentially intact. Because of its visibility the devastation of war usually appears to be more permanent than it really is. Hence the customary exaggeration of its effects. Within all reality a deep "remedial force," as Emerson called it, works its miraculous cures. Perhaps it is akin to the restorative energy that in an earlier age medical doctors called *vis medicatrix*, or internal curative force. For human things, though always fragile, are yet more resistant than we know, and despite their moribund appearances, often retain a tenacious secret vitality. Upon his return to Spain in 1946, to his surprise Ortega sensed this "underground" vitality and commented that Spain was "indecently" healthy.

Since then, mistakes have happened, fads and fanaticisms have come and gone, and much of the legacy of 1898 has been overlooked, repudiated, and forgotten. But the abiding advantage of these generations is that their astonishing work is available, brilliantly begun and brimming with genius, awaiting those endowed with the generosity of mind and spirit to bring it to further fruition.

Furthermore, in a double sense the generations of 1898 are

still at work, still advancing along the lines of free and excellent creativity begun so many years ago. To begin with, the extraordinary longevity of some of its most productive members means that what used to be called "the Generation of 1898" has now spanned the entire twentieth century and is entering the twenty-first. But the impact of departed members is hardly less. Ortega, Azorín, Unamuno, Lorca, Baroja, Valle-Inclán, and others continue to have a real presence, for they continue to be read as real persons, adding to the richness and critical mass of Spanish thought and letters during what now we ought to begin calling Spain's "Second Golden Age."

Finally, what have we discovered about Spain in all we have probed and pondered? What is the enduring sense of the world that Spain built? This will be our concluding theme.

Chapter 5:
The Spirit of Spain

A. SPANISH "STOICISM"?

Believing themselves to be the heirs of Seneca, a native of ancient Córdoba, for centuries the Spanish have taken their stoic spirit for granted. ¹ But in the light of all we have seen in Spain, do we not have reason to conclude that the Spanish differ radically from the mold of a stoic people?

Certainly we cannot deny the admiration the Spanish have always felt for Seneca (who was taken in childhood to Rome and never again resided in Hispania). Thus Quevedo, who often echoes Seneca in his Poemas morales, turns one of his apothegms—Quod unus populus eripuerit omnibus, facilius uni ab omnibus eripi posse—into a prophetic vision of the enmity that was already beginning to oppress Spain:

Y es más facil, ¡oh España!, en muchos modos,
Que lo que a todos les quitaste sola
Te puedan a ti sola quitar todos.
(And it is an easy matter; ¡oh Spain!, that in many ways,
what you alone took from all,
All may take from you alone.)
(Advertencia a España) 71, Obra poética ¹

Yet while conceding as many temperamental affinities as one may wish, we must keep in mind that even though he was born in Hispania, Seneca was not Spanish for the same, or similar, reasons that the Moors of <u>Al-Andalus</u> were not. Perhaps we could say he was proto-Spanish, for he belonged to a society that was ancestral to Spain. We could add that it was partly because of his noble doctrine—sadly often made questionable by Seneca's own dubious behavior—that Spain was destined to create one of the most original varieties of Western Christianity. In any case because of all the ancient doctrines stoicism was the most compatible with Christianity, Stoics are what the Spanish might have been if Christianity had not existed.

Late Classical people could only contemplate with heroic resignation or hand-wringing despair the decline of their ancient religions and the collapse of their civil state, the former eroded from within by philosophical doubts and the latter assaulted from without by barbarous hordes. <u>Sustine et abstine</u>, endure and renounce, the old formula of the Stoics, was a philosophy for harsh and unbelieving times. Seneca himself refined it in painful exile.

Stoicism is a morality of <u>vita minima</u>, minimal life, in which, to put it paradoxically, there is no hope of further hope. Reason, virtue, and the moral imperatives of personal life, all admirable personal qualities that the Stoics extolled and Seneca himself sometimes exemplified, resonate to nothing transcendent as the Christian faith has defined the term. Fate has the last word but not the final victory, for unlike the fatalist who bows in abject surrender to its decrees, the Stoic dies, as he has lived, in inviolable equanimity. There his story ends, and there it really begins for the Christian.

For the Christianized European had a very different view of life, one characterized by a unique and radical inclination toward the future, and beyond it, to the supra-future of the Hereafter. If the Stoic was the moral master of his finite existence, Western man is more properly the novelist of his endless life, for he must decide in this world who he will be now and forever. The setting of his story is that spiritual plane whereon occur the aesthetic, scientific, and intellectual correspondences between the human person and the Divine that are the original metaphysical core of Western art and thought. Whereas to the Stoic the world appeared to be implacably indifferent and hostile to his life, to the European and the Westerner it is redolent with the sweet scent of redemptive hope for his faith, his life, and his works. The Christian could endure the harshest life because of hope, whereas without it the Stoic could only endure in passive defiance of fate.

For this reason, the stolid equanimity with which the Stoic contemplated his own mortality resembles only superficially the imperturbable dignity with which the classic Spaniard faced death. Unlike the Christianized Spaniard, the Stoic could not know what it meant to be "proud of his soul," as Gómez de la Serna puts it, amidst even the darkest mortal trauma. The best the Stoic could do in the face of death was to stand unmoved and unyielding. On the other hand, the classic Spaniard, whose view of life is captured in the majestic <u>Coplas</u> of Jorge Manrique, died fortified not only by the further hope of a better life to come but also by the assurance that his valorous deeds would leave a worthy example for this world.

For the Stoic both life and death were equally tragic dimensions of an uncaring fate, and the only possible human dignity consisted in not being duped by it. He could only endure and renounce, determined to be as indifferent to fate as fate was to him. But for the classic Spaniard it was not a matter of years lived but of the quality of life.

As Quevedo writes:
> *Nadie contaba cuanta edad vivía,*
> *Sino de que manera ...*
> *(No one counted how long he lived but in what manner...)*

This vision of imperishable human dignity achieved its supreme expression in Spanish Christianity, but in one variant or another it was the common assumption of European life for a thousand years. The Christian conception of life, for all its lapses, infidelities, and betrayals in Spain and elsewhere, was the hopeful spiritual current that lifted European civilization, its arts, sciences, philosophies, and modes of governance to a level of unmatched superiority.

A time came, however, when Europe began to forsake the Christian vision of life. As Europeans became more rational, they could scarcely credit such an extravagantly optimistic view of human life with the added virtue of being true. Surely, they reasoned, life must be less than this, for they chose to believe in a universe that corresponded to their human reason, not to their supernatural faith. As we have seen, the medieval age of faith culminated in the genius of the Renaissance, whereas Enlightenment rationality worked toward its demise.

The unraveling began by denying the transcendent eternal life promised by Christianity. The moderns hastened to compensate mankind by promising material enrichment of earthly existence. (What I called modernity's "substitutionary idealism") This cut against the grain of the classic Spanish understanding which, newly reprised by the Generations of 1898, consisted of **ennobling** personal life. Both understandings of human life claimed happiness as their ultimate aim, but they approached it from opposite poles.

According to the substitutionary ideal or "second theory" of human life, as we called it elsewhere, happiness must surrender its transcendent attributes and take on a worldly image. Writing of the Enlightenment, Ariel and Will Durant observe: "As the educated classes surrendered their hopes of heaven they consoled themselves with earthly substitutes: the well-to-do, ignoring religious prohibitions, indulged themselves with wealth and power, women and wine and art; the commoners found solace in visions of a utopia in which the goods of the earth would be equally shared between simple and clever, weak and strong."[2]

On the other hand, the native Spanish intuition of happiness deeply indebted to Classical and Christian factors shares little with the mass-oriented notions of happiness that arose in modern times, notably from the thought of John Locke, the eighteenth-century Physiocrats, and their positivist, socialist, and Marxist heirs. (The so-called "Post-modernists" also deviate from the Modern norms of happiness but in ways radically different from the Spanish.) For the Spanish, happiness has always culminated in these twin imperatives: to live honorably and to die well as the unique person one is—and hopes to be forever. The classic Spaniard would not have disputed the ancient Greek maxim that character is destiny, only he would have his deeper conviction that worthy character itself must first be grounded in honor.

The classic Spanish conception of happiness rarely affords priority to materialism but arises instead from the radical uniqueness of the person who, like Don Quixote, knows who he is, or, more importantly, who he strives to be. Naturally the Spaniard has not been indifferent to wealth or unconcerned with poverty, but here he might agree for once with Rousseau that luxury corrupts rich and poor alike, the former by possession and the latter by covetousness. Yet in either case he is more firmly persuaded—and seldom hesitates to say so—that the truly poor in spirit are those willing to surrender honor for hope of gain or fear of loss.

B. COMPARATIVE SPIRITUAL REGISTERS

Perhaps for the reason briefly outlined above, namely, that unlike other modern peoples—the English or the Americans, for example—whose highest ideals either coincide with prior practical and economic interests or may even be derived from them, the endeavors that historically have moved the Spanish are previous to utilitarian benefits. Like Cervantes's famous knight of la Mancha, the classic Spaniard begins from an unpremeditated ideal, from a personal axiological principle, as it were, and only then does it occur to him to turn to the practical provisions and detail of his enterprise. Probably this is why to pragmatist Sansón Carrasco and his modern confreres his actions seem impulsive and ill-conceived. But the results can be astonishing as the record of Iberian conquest and exploration shows.

In contrast, in the English-speaking world the idea grows out of the experience of concrete antecedents. Think of the Common Law system of jurisprudence in the English-speaking world in which "precedents" mold juridical principles.

The Spaniard customarily deals with things and persons in the light of a prior idealism immediately or remotely rooted in Christian and chivalric ethics, while the Englishman or the American is more apt to begin, like Robinson Crusoe, with pragmatic concerns, moving toward idealism as an enlightening function of his recapitulated experience. No doubt exaggerating the matter and allowing for many exceptions, we could say that the beginning point of the one is the destination of the other; the Spaniard tends to move from the ideal to the pragmatic, the Englishman or American, from the pragmatic to the ideal. The English or the American works from concrete cases and later derives abstract principles from them. Perhaps this is why American or British idealists and moralists—Thoreau, Whitman, Wordsworth—appear to think best in the midst of quiet nature and unremarkable routine.

In matters of religious faith, the Protestant seeks the spiritual from the standpoint of his physical existence, while the Spaniard knows intuitively from the start that he is a spiritual being. His challenge is to reconcile spirit and physical life. This may be why in failure the Protestant falls back into the physical whence he started, whereas the primary impulse of the Spaniard in similar loss is to retire into the spiritual, into the devout and the mystical. Perhaps this is why the Spanish have such a heroic capacity for defeat and such profound sympathies for the vanquished. It was more than mere chance that made the most sublime figure in Spanish literature—arguably in all literature—a defeated old knight from La Mancha who in losing all won the world to himself.

Were we to extrapolate further consequences from these tendencies, probably we would find that with his eyes fixed on spiritual life, the Protestant often comes to scorn as a sinful hindrance his bodily life in this world. Hence his proclivity for dramatic conversion or, conversely and for similar causes, his equally sudden plunges into alcoholism, drugs, or sexual vices. The modern age has proved its point: the prurient is the alter ego of the puritanical.

The Spaniard's primal spirituality permeates the oppressive

facts and crushing weight of routine life and ennobles his conduct even as—especially as—all else seems lost. Hence the legendary fortitude and dignity with which the Spanish face the harshest conditions and their remarkable reactive energy whenever that faith come under jeopardy.

As for the Protestant, he tends to give testimony of his faith in works of lavish generosity. If, like John Bunyan in <u>The Pilgrim's Progress,</u> he first repudiates the world by reducing it to an allegory of wickedness, he then seeks to rescue it with works of charity and redeeming love.

I suspect this is why the English race, which historically has prided itself on its common sense and profitable exploitation of the world, has also created an astonishing number of religious sects. Despite deep doctrinal divide and obvious exceptions, English Christians have tended historically toward a puritanical squeamishness regarding the flesh and its appetites and an assumption that non-Christian humanity is fundamentally depraved and under satanic dominion.

This may explain in part the ambiguity of many Christians, especially in fundamentalist denominations, toward everything without Judeo-Christian credentials. It is a dilemma that has afflicted Christian education for centuries. For stricter believers hold much of the world and its creations to be forbidden fruit which they consume at great spiritual risk to themselves. Taken to an extreme—and naturally extremes always are—not only the pagan works of antiquity but also important theories and creations of the modern mind become by default the intellectual patrimony of the unbeliever and the agnostic.

This leads to a startling paradox that afflicts all Christianity to some extent, but especially its Protestant branches: sin appears to confer freedom while belief seems to curtail it. In a parody of the Biblical promise of truthful freedom, this theology would have us believe that as we come to know the Truth, it will restrict us. Probably nothing could make the sinful life more attractive. In any case, we note an odd circularity in these English-speaking interpretations of Christianity. To those lands where once the English or the Americans ventured for gain, thither they returned with the Gospel, not to set up an empire of men but to preach with equal zeal the Kingdom of God.

Whereas the Protestant believer and perhaps most Christians generally imagine Heaven to be unimaginably—and thus frighteningly—different from this life (so much so that most vastly prefer to remain in this world as long as they can), the Spaniard appears more inclined to understand the hereafter as an essential continuity with the life he has lived here. He sees in this life the prelude to the next, or to look at it from the other side, the next life will be the fulfillment and perfection of this one. And unlike the Protestant who assumes that his immortal life will begin only after his personal death, **the Spaniard, like the great Mystics his race has produced, senses that he lives already in eternity**. Hence the Protestant tendency to devalue earthly existence in favor of the unknowable life to come, and the counter impulse—with many lapses, we must admit—of the Spaniard to live more deeply this mortal life precisely because it is the opening act to an immortal drama already begun.

Always ambivalent toward the flesh, the Protestant clings to the promise that God will save his soul. On the other hand, the Spaniard is more likely to hope for his personal salvation, that is, not just of his soul but of the whole person that he is. Hence Unamuno's scant interest in the mere immortality of his soul and his passionate hunger to live forever as Miguel de Unamuno. This irrational but humanly understandable yearning for integral personal continuity—Spinoza's famous *connatus*—constitutes the "agony," or struggle, of Unamunean Christianity.

Radicalized by this original severing of his being which has appeared as a series of dualities variously expressed—body/soul, materiality/spirit, matter/mind somata/psyche, etc.—modern and Protestant mankind, like Humpty-Dumpty in the nursery rhyme, yearns as much for the plenary reintegration of his person as he despairs of achieving it in today's world. T. S. Eliot writes in "Burn Norton" that modern mankind is

Caught in the form of limitation
Between un-being and being

Unlike modernized man, whose life is fractured like the chaotic reflections of a broken mirror, the Spaniard has been characterized by an un-modern insistence on the seamless integrity of his person in this world and the next. For all its distortions—its *esperpentos*—his spiritual mirror is not yet broken. Perhaps this is why at the psychological and spiritual levels he neither wallows nor revels in the extreme existential <u>angst</u> common in the modern Western world. (In Spanish novels one sometimes senses that these states—*de rigueur* since the advent of the modern psychological novel—must be contrived by the author and thus represent an artificial and unconvincing distortion of character.) On a mundane level the Spaniard seldom needs psychiatry, nor is he given to the kind of spectacular changes in marriage, career, friends, religion, residence, etc. that we find in Protestant life. Naturally, the Spaniard is as susceptible as anyone else to the inherent ills of the human condition and his grief runs as deep in tragic moments. But just as he resists the random fragmentation of his life, so he is less likely to alter the general coordinates of his destiny. (it is revealing in this regard that until very recent times the Spanish referred to a job or a career as a *destino* (destiny) and clung to it even when life offered them better alternatives.)

C. LITERARY CONSTANTS

For reasons that will become clearer, it is important to point out certain literary modalities associated with these two vital postures: the "modern," or Protestant" on the one hand, and its alter ego (for both derive from the same sources), the Spanish or "Catholic," on the other. Unlike literatures of "modern" or Protestant ancestry, the richness of Spanish literature does not depend primarily on psychological subtleties, nor for that matter on ideas as such, but on an incomparable biographical profundity, or to use a term alluded to earlier, on its "human depth." <u>Don Quixote</u>, for instance, is as sparse in explicit "ideas" and theories as it is rich in human profundity. (And to be truthful about it, many of the ideas we do find are intellectual commonplaces of that age.) As a result, whereas other modern Western literatures have left us celebrated types—Hamlet, Phèdre, Othello, Robinson Crusoe, Faust, Julien Sorel, Père Goriot, Emma Bovary, etc.—or unforgettable stereotypes—Monsieur Jourdain, Tartuffe, Candide, Pangloss, Jacques the Fatalist, Monsieur Homais, Ebenezer Scrooge, etc.—, none has matched Spanish letters in the creation of archetypes —Don Quixote, Sancho Panza, Don Juan, the Pícaro, and only slightly less renowned, Dulcinea, Celestina, Segismundo.

According to an ancient cliché, Spanish letters are somewhat deficient in imagination but excel in realism. But to stop there is to fall short of the truth. What we find among Spanish writers is not an imaginative deficiency but another kind of imagination, not the fanciful creations of J. R. R. Tolkien, or an H.G. Wells but what Julián Marías calls "concrete imagination," which we could define as the ability to take full possession of the real. It is an error to assume that realism is merely the transcription or imitation of reality, and those who subscribe to this mistaken notion usually give us a distorted reality. On the contrary, nothing is harder to imagine than the concrete, especially the humanly concrete, for we are customarily persuaded by its illuminated surfaces and visible, tangible qualities and prejudiced against its unseen depths, to say nothing of its latent structures we know as possibility and potential.

Although it takes us beyond the range of this book, it is fascinating to contemplate for a moment the probable analogies between the "concrete imagination" of the Spanish and the historical realities for which they are noted: the first modern State and many of its institutions—monarchy, the military, new forms of diplomacy, etc., the creation of the New World and the trans-European supernation known as "the Spains," explorations and circumnavigation of the globe, the first <u>Weltpolitik</u> since the <u>Pax Romana</u>, the modern novel, unique forms of drama, and arguably the most dynamic form of Western Christianity—the Mystics, new orders, etc. In all cases, it was not a matter of first developing theories, treatises, and ideal models of these things, as the Enlightenment thinkers would do later. Rather, the creation or invention of concrete realities in nearly all cases either preceded or coincided with theoretical constructs. To illustrate a point, for the Spanish, theory has been a product of, not a blueprint for, action.

Unquestionably the soliloquy is one of the glories of English letters. (in the novel it has become universally known as "interior monologue" popularized by James Joyce but with antecedents in Sterne.) The peerless example is Hamlet, but Robinson Crusoe's intermittent and implicit soliloquy is no less remarkable in a more diffuse way. (Even after the subsequent arrival of "Friday" no sustained dialogue between equals occurs. He remains an imperfectly delineated character and a weakness of the novel.)

It is true that there are also celebrated soliloquies in Spanish literature. Think of Segismundo's famous solitary utterances. But whereas such solitude to Calderón appears to be an abnormal state of human life, to the English, American, or German writer it is more frequently the plenitude of being. As Sir Edward Dyer (1543-1607) puts it,

My mind to me a kingdom is;
Such perfect joy therein I find
That it excels all other bliss
Which God or Nature hath assigned.
(My Mind to me a Kingdom is)

It is a commonplace that Mediterranean peoples have always been at their scintillating best in dialogue and human society. (It is said that Diderot's works were mere scraps left over from much more creative conversations in eighteenth-century Parisian salons). On the other hand, Northern peoples—cf. Thoreau,—tend to think and enjoy their best and most beautiful thoughts alone. Greek philosophers defined and defended their systems amidst the chaotic human traffic of the agora; Kant walked along the quiet streets of Königsberg sunk in what Wordsworth called "The self-sufficing power of solitude." Need we wonder why German philosophy, suspicious and wary of the gregarious outer world, always gave ascendancy to the solitary conscience and stubbornly tried to subsume the external world in it? And should it surprise us that to garrulously communicative Southerners the taciturn Northerners so often seem personally inferior to their works?

For his part, condemned to a monstrous solitude and unaware of his real circumstances, Segismundo—or Calderón—feels the Mediterranean person's full horror of his tragic condition made worse because he does not understand it. (For other reasons that have little to do with solitude Hamlet also suffers the distorting hallucinations of an imagination run amok.) At the nadir of despair, Segismundo proclaims that man's greatest misfortune is to have been born, a heresy that Calderón eventually rectifies.

Until recently the tendency of Northern races toward aesthetic and psychological hermeticism culminated in lyric poetry, the supreme literary form of the solitary mind. Think of the love sonnets of Shakespeare, the philosophical lyricism of Gray and Wordsworth, the Romanticism of Byron, Shelley, and Keats, the metaphysical poems of T.S. Eliot and Yeats. Perhaps this is one explanation for the mysterious fact that the English and their cultural progeny, who pride themselves above all on their common sense and pragmatic approach to life, who barely tolerate poetry as a profitless whim, have produced some of the world's most beautiful verse. They are most comfortable with the silently inanimate, including abstract ideas, which they manipulate at will, and least so with other persons who talk back and who possess an arcane inner life and the possibility of multiple relationships.

Unlike the self-conscious and self-engrossed peoples of Northern extraction with their legendary tendency toward psychological and philosophical introspection and—frequently—spiritual implosion, the Spaniard, the Mediterranean, is much more inclined to life as dialogue, which is the primary form of altruism and the precondition of all human relationships. (A curious notion lingers to this day among intellectuals of Protestant extraction that the more one talks about ideas, the less likely one is to write them later. Talk, they assume, is frivolous and mere taciturnity is often thought to be a virtue. Ideas are considered to be among the most private of one's parts and only in published form are they deemed fit for public scrutiny. For his part, the Mediterranean person is more inclined to assume that ideas need the preliminary grind and polish of dialogue, the better to write them later.)

Surprisingly indifferent to the abstract public domain (which unlike mass manifestations is invisible and unseen), the Spaniard compensates by an affinity for the social. The Northerner seldom understands this dichotomy and upon seeing the apparent fragility of the public sector in Hispanic societies, reasons from his own circumstances that the entire culture is in imminent danger of collapse. And indeed, it probably would be if it happened in countries of northern ancestry where the public sector occupies the prime terrain of life. Hence the constant reminders by English-speaking "experts" of the calamitous conditions and probable ruination of the Hispanic world. Of course, they are wrong, and the end never quite comes.[3] For the Northerner fails to grasp that whereas the *res publica* tends to be secondary in Hispanic life, Hispanic societies themselves are resilient, strong, and spontaneous. If there were a way to measure the median level of happiness in Spain and other Hispanic countries, I suspect it would be surprisingly high.

But while dialogue in the sense described above naturally includes ordinary conversation, it also implies a certain way of understanding and organizing reality—an implicit metaphysics, if you will—in which mute and humble things also have their say. For the Spaniard it seems that nothing is fully real until it can be said, and nothing fully true until it is said well. For the Spaniard senses—even when he cannot make sense of it—that far from being an objective commodity passively waiting for us to discover it, truth, as Machado said, must also be created. Here religious faith and implicit Spanish metaphysics veer in accord, for truth appears as a telling just as theologically Truth manifests as *Logos*.[4] He would not deny that the power of truth is primarily redemptive, only he would probably add, as Ortega hinted, that in order to save us by its power, truth must first seduce by its beauty. For faith comes from hearing—*Fides ex auditu*.

Probably it is no accident that the literary creation we call the modern novel, a genre of dialogue, originated in Spain. The fact that in recent times dialogue in the novel has been disrupted by authorial, ideological, and psychological intrusions and distortions of one kind or another probably represents a degeneration of the novel form. With other aims in mind, Ortega once described the "dehumanization" of the novel, but the truth is that in its original dialogical form it is the most "humanized" of all the literary genres. For dialogue occurs only in personal proximity. It abolishes distance and time—it is always in the contextual present tense—and puts us in the immediate presence of the characters. Cervantes does not simply tell us about Don Quixote and Sancho; instead, he keeps us within earshot of them so that we can listen in on their conversation as we travel with them across an ideal landscape that becomes real to us as it is humanized and reported in their dialogues. And the auditory is complemented by the visual clarity of the Cervantine style. As Flaubert writes admiringly, *Comme on voit ces routes d'Espagne qui ne sont nulle part décrites!* (How one sees those roads of Spain that are nowhere described!). [5]

By a curious reversal it is we, persons of flesh and blood, whose presence is spectral. Our ideal presence reminds us that in each generation the reader—the silent third participant—changes and this successively recasts the dialogue and the visual panorama in a new context and perspective that allow the work to retain its "classic" force in each succeeding era. But though new, the continuity remains. For what is humanly relevant for one age vibrates sympathetically with the true concerns of other times.

Probably realizing that a solitary Don Quixote would be an inadequate literary—and human—basis for the novel, Cervantes abbreviates his knight's first sally and the second time sends him forth accompanied for good by the sturdy Sancho. Had Don Quixote been English or German, very likely he and Sancho would have fused into a single character—perhaps a personage resembling a Faust or a Hamlet. [6] And it is conceivable that if he had been French, Cervantes would have reduced them to caricatures in the lineage of Gargantua and Candide, perhaps with similar burlesque overtones in the Gallic style of a Voltaire or Diderot. In any case, had they been born in other climes, Don Quixote and Sancho might well have been simple stereotypes, for the rule holds that people—both fictional and fleshly—appear as stereotypes when deprived of their biographical depth. Only beyond the narration of ideas and the portrayal of psychology do we enter the biographical depths of personhood. [7]

It is precisely because of this indivisible human depth that both Don Quixote the man and <u>Don Quixote</u> the novel prove so resistant to the literary reductionism we call analysis.

D. MASTER TROPES: SPAIN AND DON QUIXOTE

The preceding comparisons form a context within which to make some summary observations about Spain. I shall center these remarks on the two master tropes generally favored by the Generations of 1898 in their "rediscovery" of Spain: Castile and Don Quixote. My emphasis will be on the latter. I would be tempted to subtitle these the "real" and "fictional" dimensions of Spain were it not that the lines are now so blurred between them that it would be a distraction to try to redraw them. The Generations of 1898 went to great lengths to vindicate the right of fiction to claim a stake in reality and their arguments are still convincing enough to be respected.

Earlier we noted how the Generations of 1898 set out to rediscover—and so to recover—Spain in its most elemental presence: the landscape, the people, and the past. Two preliminary features of this quest require our attention here. The first is that the unsatisfactory nature of Spanish history itself impelled poets and philosophers into non-textual or extra-historical modes of recovery. The Spain they sought, the Spain they intuited, either had not been written or written poorly, so that it was necessary to search for it not in tomes nor yet in mere apostrophic or Romantic divinization of the landscape but in the enduring relationships that bound land to man. Here, in these abiding relationships, Unamuno discovered his "intrahistory," and here also Azorín, Machado, and Ortega achieved a post-Romantic and ultimately post-Modernistic balance of aesthetic sentiment and factual reality. For it was not simply a matter of annotating in positivistic or phenomenological fashion what appeared before them—the telluric starkness of Castilian villages, fields, and backroads—but of reinjecting as though by alchemical magic renewed human life into the moldering ruins of a land that perhaps for centuries had slumbered in a dreamless sleep.

The other point is that unlike most quests that begin with liberal quantities of good spirits—the perennial optimism of beginnings—this one was conceived in pessimism. Yet to understand this pessimism rightly is, or so I believe, to go a long way toward deciphering the enigma of Spain. For while most pessimism arises from a fear of things becoming worse, the version we find in the Generations of 1898 is a lament that things were not better.

It would a mistake, therefore, to think that the rediscovery of Spain involved only a search for its historical and geographical reality. It is true that the longing for a new style to replace the predominant sensibilities of the Restoration was expressed by the Generations of 1898 as a determination to communicate with a Spain that transcended its "official" political versions. But beyond this celebrated declaration, one that depended too much perhaps on the very thing it opposed and was in danger for a time of becoming simply an anti-Restoration rhetoric, a more ambitious quest began for another Spain that had never appeared in historical form but which had always accompanied history as an ideal of what could have been. The "yearning for heights" that Azorín spoke of must be understood, therefore, as the spiritual context from which a greater Spain, unrealized but suggestively real nonetheless, might begin to take form. The fact that these

Generations of 1898 were living with their mind and body in Spain but with one foot already in its ideal version introduced a note of discontent and restlessness—of *agonía*—that was worlds removed from the vaunted Spanish "stoicism."

But this virtuality must not be thought of as simply a suggestion of what could evolve into reality or stand as an unreal alternative to the intolerable Spain in which they had been born. The Generations of 1898 resisted such convenient idealism even as they gave voice to it, and they were not, generally speaking, overly enthusiastic about Hegelian or Darwinian notions of an unfolding or evolution of something implicit or latent from the start. The very unreality of the Spain they intuited meant to them that it first had to be created, or at least recreated from the raw materials of desultory history. For them the reality they found was itself a fiction despite its tangible concreteness. In their acute dichotomization of the world, they ostensibly resembled the Romantics. But with a difference: whereas the Romantics generally fled from the real world in search of the ideal, the first Generations of 1898 looked beyond their world in order to discover the superior dimensions of reality.

They also echoed the Romantics in their metaphorical ingenuity and thematic sensitivity, yet here also they had other aims in mind. To the Romantics the real world had been a metaphorical springboard to the ideal worlds of sentiment; for the Generations of 1898 the virtual was an inseparable dimension of reality itself. The difference, which may seem semantically insignificant, is far reaching, for it informs their art and their vision of the world. Philosophically this vision culminated as a metaphysical doctrine in Ortegan thought and in this formulation became a component of Spanish intellectualism and letters that in subsequent times could be ignored only at the risk of archaic recidivism. (The fact that in recent years these relapses have happened makes the creativity of Ortegan thought all the more evident by contrast.) It consisted in the premise that reality, and particularly human reality, exceeds the sum of its contents, or to put it negatively, that metaphysics, which devolves on a theory of human life, is not identical to classical ontology, or the science of being, as philosophers had assumed for centuries, nor is it reducible to biology or somatic functions as modern science has presupposed.

As we have seen before, the first Generations of 1898 defiantly proclaimed their youthful determination to develop an anti-Restoration style. Here we may remind ourselves anew that the "style" they sought must be understood as a way of life within which literary style is one of several subsets. But their youthful hubris may cause us to overlook the more important fact that once this was done, and done rather handily, they turned in their maturity to the more challenging task of transcending the larger cultural matrix from which not only the Restoration but the whole of modernity derived. The crisis of the Restoration at the national level led them inexorably to the universal crisis of modern rationalism. In time the style they developed to replace the Restoration became a challenge to modernity itself. We shall come back to this theme.

They would not fall into the same trap as the old Romantics and see their best efforts overwhelmed by the resurgence in stronger forms of what they had opposed. Romanticism began as a self-conscious revolt against rationalism, narrowly personified initially in Rousseau's break with Voltaire and the *Philosophes*. Indeed, it is an irony that the rational neatness and contrapuntal nature of the Romantic Movement has always been one of its most appealing and teachable features. Before 1761 the Enlightenment from Bayle and Buffon to Voltaire and Diderot had been an age of reason; after the publication of Rousseau's Julie ou la nouvelle Héloïse it became increasingly a Romantic proclamation of the rights of sentimentality.

Yet we need to keep in mind that some of its early defenders described Romanticism as a superior form of "realism" in which without denying reason, feelings were acknowledged as components of reality. This concession was the first step toward the modern discoveries and refinements of the psychological and subconscious levels of life.[8]

The problem with Romanticism proper was that it did not go far enough. To the end it remained a parasitical movement that lacked a sound theoretical foundation on which to sustain what it proposed and to overcome what it opposed. In reality, the great Romantics were mere renegades of rationalism whose mode of being was understandable only in view of the rationality they flouted. No wonder the old rationalism, metamorphosed by science into nineteenth-century realism with its positivistic cast and impressive advances, its "progress," soon recaptured the territory it had lost to Romanticism. By 1850 Romanticism resembled nothing so much as a revolutionary interlude, a brief pause in the march toward rational order and progress.

But the return to Castilian roots alone was incomplete; without the epiphanous human appearance it would remain inert, telluric, essentially infra-human. We could say, therefore, that it was the stage setting on which Don Quixote and Sancho would perform a ritual of human destiny. The Generations of 1898 were sensitized to this drama to a degree that no Spaniards before them had been, for they were convinced in different ways that in their bizarre quest the old knight and his squire were acting out the Spanish mode of being, what Unamuno would call "the tragic sense of life."

It was a question, therefore, of understanding this essential Quixotic being. But which form do we mean? For some, including Unamuno and Madariaga, it was personified in Don Quixote himself. Unamuno resurrects Cervantes's hero and sends him riding off in anti-rational and neo-medieval defiance of modernity, while Madariaga tries to make him a spokesman for rational modernism.

The Unamunean Don Quixote was not merely another doctrine to be added to the series that Europe had produced in modern times but a radical negation of all rationalistic doctrine. It was to philosophy what anarchy was to politics. Unamuno himself described it as "poetry" or "phantasmagoria." In any case, the mission of this resurrected Don Quixote was not to reason with the Sanson Carrascos of modern science and thought, which would be to pose the questions of human destiny at an inferior level, but to cry out in a spiritual desert littered with the ruined dreams of modernity. There one seldom finds peace, Unamuno admonishes us, but may experience a hard-won glory.

For Ortega, on the other hand, to attempt to emulate Don Quixote himself would amount to what he called "an invitation to an absurd existence," or perhaps to a "biographical madness," in the words of Julián Marías. For this reason, Ortega prefers the proto-Quixotic vision of Cervantes. To put it another way, Ortega finds in the way Cervantes approaches reality the essential and proper Spanish "style," understood in the all-embracing sense that we saw earlier. As Ortega comments a bit enigmatically: "If we knew clearly what the style of Cervantes consists of, the way in which he approaches things, we would have achieved everything. For in these spiritual summits there reigns an indissoluble solidarity, and a poetic style bears within itself a philosophy, a morality, a science, and a politics."[9]

We are still far from formal doctrine. Cervantes never claimed to be a philosopher. Yet he does something that we could describe as proto-philosophical: he allows life to function in such a way that prior to its metaphysical formulation in Ortegan philosophy, the components of a future theory of the Spanish mode of being are already mobilized in their literary form. This is why we find the nucleus of Ortega's doctrine in <u>Meditations on Quixote</u>, even though he seems to talk of nearly everything in that work except Don Quixote and Sancho.

Although Unamunean Quixoticism stands as the most strident challenge to modern science and reason, which Unamuno summarily and contemptuously dismissed as "Kultura," the quixotic doctrine we find in Ortega is much more radical. There is an obvious difference of strategy. Unamuno attacks modernity frontally and from without, much as Don Quixote launched his celebrated assault on the windmills. The result is equally ineffective, for despite Unamuno's heroic challenge, the foundations of modernity remain intact.

Ortega tries a different tactic. He undermines the very pillars on which modernity rests—Cartesian rationalism, the rule of mass-man, the preeminence of the political, the predominant artistic and philosophic genres and forms. Unlike Unamuno for whom the Quixotic was an archaic defiance of rationalistic thought, a defiance that consisted of declaiming rather than proving the superiority of the irrational, Ortega found in the

Quixote, though not in the life of Don Quixote, the coordinates for a new rationalism and a new metaphysics. For Ortega the solution to the crisis of reason was not an absurd irrationalism but a higher and all-embracing form of reason itself, one that turned out to be identical with life and not merely its ally in a futile antirational sally against modernity.

This new reason involved more than the simple substitution of one form of rationalism for another. The most obvious trait of life, so evident as to seem trivial, is that **it goes on. Life is not merely a definable thing that is, but an indefinable person who lives.** But the consequences are anything but trivial. Because life is a temporal succession of dramatic scenes, its dialectical form is necessarily narrative and dialogical in nature. Life is "scenic" in a theatrical sense; one scene happens, another replaces it and passes in turn, and we understand them in temporal juxtaposition. We can say that at any given juncture mortal life presents itself as a task that allows no delays. It is always happening here and now, imperfective and unfinished and hence unrelentingly needful and urgent. We always find ourselves in a certain situation that we understand only in reference to others, past and possible. This is why its story is not a tale just for others but for us, so that we may understand ourselves and make our way through the world.

Yet even though life's inherent dynamism is historically and biographically scenic and situational as we have described it, this movement does not happen in isolation. Our life happens in time, and time's only manifestation consists of going on. Yet we do not go alone. We saw earlier that the all-embracing form of reason that Ortega called vital reason does not work in abstract space but instead implies or, better, implicates an intricate network of human significances that are historical and virtual. Man is his factual history and physical being, but where these stop, he goes on, for his reality also consists in his further possibilities and impossibilities. And these he must have constantly at his disposal in art, ethics, law, religion, and science. This, in sum, is the nucleus of the Ortegan way of thinking. But how does this relate to the Quixotic vision of life?

E. QUIXOTIC LIFE AND THE WESTERN MIND

In startling, sometimes pathetic, and often humorous contrast to their "real" circumstances, Don Quixote and Sancho live and act on a plane defined by *ilusión* (in both the illusory and the positive way the term can be understood in Spanish). We must not take too seriously Sancho's celebrated "realism," for he too is motivated by ambitions that for all their humble or pecuniary nature are no less ideal for him. Don Quixote is moved by a profoundly simple but imponderably deep conviction that life is immeasurably rich and worthwhile, that it is worth the trouble to strive to the utmost, to achieve, to seek the fame and glory of the chivalric code, even though the effort brings sufferings and hardships. Nothing external impels him to undertake the task. **He understands that honor, glory, and morality are gifts we give ourselves.** There are, therefore, no convincing external "causes" of his transformation, least of all the stated reason that he read too many novels of chivalry. Here we suspect that Cervantes is either having fun at our expense or for a moment himself fails to understand Don Quixote.

Con poco me contento, aunque deseo mucho (I am content with little, although I desire much), says Don Quixote, unlike the stoic who is satisfied with little because he desires little. He shows above all that our first impulses, the ones that move us toward achievement and sustain us in our trajectories, are not primarily volitional, materialistic, or rationalistic, but desiderative. We are moved in the first instance by our desires, in their strongest and purest form, by our loves.

This motivation and the corresponding tilt toward the unrealized and perhaps the unreachable, in a word, toward the future one creates and not its fatalistic alter ego, are the same traits we identified in a previous chapter as the distinguishing features of European and Western mankind. Madariaga saw in the person of Don Quixote the prototypical European. I agree with his conclusions but not for the reasons this respected writer adduces. For while modern rationalistic thought depends on abstract and atemporal logic, the "reason" we find in Don Quixote is more akin to protean human wisdom. His is the reason that life itself becomes as we live it.

Although he defends personal liberty, not for a moment does he do so for the sake of any sort of modern democratic equality of the human condition. Instead, he acts on an opposing principle: he strives for the personal superiority and nobility one achieves only through valor and heroic deeds. These reflect not the democratic prudence of modern man, but the high morality, discipline, and courage of the person determined to rise above the common, especially the common humanity one would otherwise be.

As modern people we are not troubled by the fact that in our age, man is free only as far and as long as the State and its magistrates guarantee him the constitutional and legal right to freedom. Nor does it seem to bother us that our freedom is provisional and not personal at all, for where the constitutional power or benevolence of the State ends our freedom abruptly ceases. Our kind of freedom does not emanate from us but from an outside source and depends on its existence and power. Roman right depended on Roman might and ended when Rome fell.

On the other hand, far from being a generic right subject to the whim of an external power, Don Quixote's freedom is truly personal, everywhere undiminished in principle because he bears it with him and aims to defend it wherever he goes. Whether in fact he is able to do so is an altogether secondary matter.

Sprawled on the ground, his body battered and sore, Don Quixote says, "I know who I am." But who is he really? To the modern mind obviously he is Alonso Quijano, or Quesada, or maybe Quijana. (Had he lived in more recent times his identification documents would have settled the matter as far as society and the State are concerned.) Acting on this rational assumption his friends, including the much-maligned Sansón Carrasco, try to get him to return to his village roots. To them Don Quixote of la Mancha will always be a joke.

Moreover, there is an awkward moment in the narrative when Cervantes seems unsure of the real surname of his character, just as in the earlier context he will not tell us the name of Alonso's village.

Is this a simple lapse on the part of the author? Many have thought so and some have called <u>Don Quixote</u> the most carelessly written of the world's great masterpieces. They may be right, of course, but let us consider another possibility. First, Don Quixote refuses to limit himself to his factual past. He cannot bring himself to continue being the simple villager he has always been and whom everybody thinks they know. For this reason, the facts of his former life, even if we concede their accuracy, are of a decidedly secondary importance. Instead of being an example of Cervantes's supposed carelessness, they may be instead an ingenious stratagem of the great novelist. For without eliminating the facts surrounding Alonso Quijano, or Quesada, or Quijana, by means of these ambiguities and uncertain references, Cervantes disqualifies them so that the futuristic, projective, and "illusioned" life of the man who would be Don Quixote becomes the focus of the novel. Attention shifts from past to future. It does not much matter who this local neighbor Alonso was or was not because from now on as Don Quixote he will define himself by the life he imagines and projects before him.

Abruptly, improbably, scandalously, the man once known as Alonso begins his ascent to another level of human magnitude: he will forge his own destiny. He has inclined sharply and deliberately toward the future with a corresponding release of his past. To put it another way, the spiritual dimension of his life has been energized by what we described earlier as "the possible future," and this frees him from both an unremarkable past and the routine future his life would have been had he remained in his unnamed town. **In the purest European spirit, he abandons his fate and sets out futuristically to create his destiny.**

Why does this change appeal to us? We understand the skepticism of Alonso's neighbors. For we tend to be as wisely prudent in our advice to others as we are broadly indulgent with ourselves. Furthermore, the same people who fascinate us in fiction—a Don Quixote, an Emma Bovary—would not be our friends in everyday life. Yet even as the rational neighbors claim our understanding, they fail to earn our sympathies, for these remain with Alonso—Don Quixote.

In his extravagant way—and the extravagance is all the more useful to demonstrate the point—Don Quixote personifies the human condition itself, at least the Western version of that condition. In our lesser moments we may choose to live life as if it were merely a matter of unremarkable continuity, and to the degree we do so, we allow a certain falsification to settle over us. For in reality the simple but tremendous fact remains that life is an unfinished task and thus a creative obligation. Throughout life we seek to complete the task of becoming the person we are called—mysteriously called—to be. The habits, repetitions, and social customs that mark our lives with various levels of comfort and routine also conceal its unavoidably perilous emerging character. Despite all the ways we disguise the fact, life remains a risky venture, an *ad*-venture, a journey into the unexpected and the unpredictable.

Don Quixote fascinates because he circumvents the subterfuges that conceal our real condition and reveals the pure dynamism of human life. **This is why for all their rich pathos and entertaining qualities, Don Quixote's subsequent deeds and mishaps do not themselves constitute the essential drama of the novel. Rather they are reflections and effects of the prior and deeper drama of human life striving for definition and significance, which Don Quixote understands primarily as the worthy and noble quest for honor and glory in the name of his lady Dulcinea.**

Thus, the erstwhile villager Alonso is "reborn" as Don Quixote. But the traditional terms must be inverted in order to understand the transformation. It was not that the real person Alonso falsified his life and pretended to be someone he was not; instead, he sloughed off the falsified person he had always been so as to become the person he was called to be. Alonso experiences a "renaissance," a rebirth in the original and true sense of the word, and the experience reminds us that the life we have always led, the life of routine, may be the most alien to our true calling.

Life consists in our yearning to become our true selves. Yet we must admit in this same context that if villager Alonso was an imperfect version of the man, initially Don Quixote is no less so. His claims are preposterous and unsubstantial, for he has not yet conquered foes and gained fame, nor even declared loyalty to his lady. Were we to decide on this basis alone, we would have to admit that his friends and critics were right. From this we derive a conclusion that Ortega would convert to doctrine: human reality is not a matter of material essence, not a question of what we are, but of our trajectory. The age-old question, what is man?, is wrongly worded and therefore has always led to erroneous answers. For it is not **what** we are—biology, psyche, psychology, substance, *esse*—but **who** we are, or better, who we are becoming. Human life reveals itself only in process, as a trajectory, or series of trajectories, we call biography. And in its passing life mobilizes the muted world in a certain way and allows it to manifest. As Ortega demonstrated so masterfully in <u>Meditations on Quixote</u>, the world and I need each other in order to be. In Ortega's imperishable expression: I am I and my circumstance, and if I do not save it I cannot save myself. Seen from another perspective, human reality is always temporally and historically involved, and futuristically inclined. This is why human life cannot be reduced to definition but must be understood as biography.

Alonso's conversion to Don Quixote reminds us of the stupendous human capacity for repentance, the possibility of making a radical change of direction in both the secular and religious sense. It is the ultimate human triumph over the dreary fatalism that would condemn us without appeal to unhappiness.

As a knight errant, Alonso takes on a new name so as to initiate his new life. But as we saw earlier, it is a name singularly devoid of meaning; his is a life yet without deeds and laurels of victory. No rational person can take him seriously, for rationality must be anchored in the tangible. Lacking a past, he can only look to the future for fulfillment. No ancient attachments bind him; no old habits veto his primary impulses. But what this gives him in the form of potentiality, it removes in experience.

Like a lesser Adam, Don Quixote begins a life that consists almost entirely of anticipated possibilities. By choice or not, he remembers almost nothing and thus can look forward to everything. For a few moments this allows him to experience freedom in its primordial existential fullness. It is the high privilege reserved only for the heroic life. For if all human life consists partly of its unrealized futuristic dimensions, in the case of Don Quixote, this is true to a superlative degree. The content of his life and the significance of his name depend on deeds not yet done.

This is why his greatest struggle is not against real or imaginary enemies but against his own unsubstantial condition as Don Quixote. He is barely and precariously himself, and this suggests that so is everything human.

Don Quixote becomes, therefore, the archetypal Western man who lives in radical and "illusioned" inclination toward the future, who strives to forge his life and fortune—in a word, his happiness—in view of the future's suggestive horizons. His life is a "felicitary" quest, not a state of achieved and finished being. Perhaps more than any other person in Western literature, Don Quixote embodies the ontological tension, the "agony," of the Western understanding of life. And it is this human depth, not his symbolic or metaphorical significance, that has rendered him immortal. For we must not forget that it was not Don Quixote who died but Alonso the returning villager, not the spirit but the body that perished.

In his ontological quest to be himself Don Quixote insists on freedom, for this futuristic projection requires it. Or to state it conversely, life without this "illusioned" inclination toward the future can hardly be free. But above all, we must add that the most intense freedom occurs when we commit ourselves with all our heart to what—or better, to whom—we truly love. For love has the greatest affinity for the future.

Thus, we can say that freedom culminates in love, which in a paradoxical turn becomes voluntary devotion and servitude. It may be, as Antonio Machado says, that nobody chooses his love, and in this sense it is inevitable. Yet it is within our power to accept or reject it as our destiny, as our calling, and either bet our life on it or hold back in half-hearted resolve. But if our wholeheartedness in love is dangerous, reluctance is even costlier, for experience proves over and again that neither love nor freedom is compatible with such reluctance. Those who would save their life by this strategy will assuredly lose it in the long run, and with it the love and freedom that give it meaning.

No wonder the fearful and calculating modern spirit enjoys less and less freedom and finds love ever more elusive. Stultified by routine and overwhelmed by tensions, modern people will not risk long and dramatic commitments in love and marriage. Their real love is economic and personal security for which they are willing to sacrifice time, spontaneity, and freedom. Paradoxically, in their zeal to live well, modern people voluntarily condemn themselves to living poorly. In order not to expose themselves to economic uncertainty or—even worse—to the social disapproval of certain individuals or groups, modern people are ever more willing to mouth popular opinions and adopt faddish styles regardless of how repulsive these may be to their nature. In other words, they become formally irresponsible, because they are afraid to take responsibility for themselves, for their true thoughts and deepest yearnings.

This should not be taken to mean that modern people are merely indifferent to things in, say, the stoic manner. Habitual denial of their true feelings may lead to a deadening of sensibilities and increasingly we see such apparent examples, but usually we find people to be concerned about a multitude of things, yet with the pessimistic certainty that they are powerless to remedy them. The modern zeal for security thus manifests itself in a thousand fears and frets, for like all fearful people, the moderns are condemned to suffer everything they dread, occasionally in fact, always in fancy.

Still, we must confess they have a point. As Don Quixote soon discovers, fortune and fate are not in our hands. Our life quest becomes at once an adventure in which chance and circumstance—what Don Quixote calls the "enchanters"—may snatch away happiness and plunge us into misfortune. But he goes on to say that it is impossible for them to take from us our "striving and spirit."

This means that when all is said and done, we shall have been the masters only of what we have earnestly desired and wholeheartedly striven to achieve. Unamuno understood this very well when he wrote that we shall be judged not for who we have been but for who we have tried to be.

Because Don Quixote is the archetype of the futuristically striving European spirit, he becomes the living embodiment of life's terrible and tender fragility. Even though we modern readers are more likely than our ancestors to take pity on the old knight's physical decrepitude, we still laugh at the spectacle of one so weak striving heroically to right wrongs and do glorious deeds. With the advantage of dramatic irony and realistic experience, we know in advance that the world will trample him underfoot and declare his dreams insane.

Fortunately, Don Quixote is innocent of our cynical knowledge. He is a new person, a man reborn, and the world in which he psychically resides has been reborn with him. For the experiences, the people, the relationships he knew as Alonso remain ascribed to that abandoned life. His story, his life, begins not with his dubious existence as Alonso but with his epiphanous metamorphosis and emergence as Don Quixote. The facts of his earlier existence are not the truth of his new life. **He is a man without having been a child.** He recounts no adolescence; he tells us of no parent or sibling; he knows no binding commitments to friends or family. He is neither burdened nor guided by the limits and lessons of common sense. His aspirations are native and naïve, as yet untrimmed by experience, and his life is as close as one can come to a pure, free, and spontaneous relationship with the world.

Through it all only his inchoate love survives the transformation, **which suggests that Alonso was already becoming Don Quixote long before the fact.** And just as he is reborn as Don Quixote, so the seemingly drab Aldonza Lorenzo is also alchemically transmuted by his love into the sublime Dulcinea.

But we must be careful not to dismiss this vision of Dulcinea as a mere delusional aberration. For she stands as a splendid example of the hidden beauty of humble things. For their apparent mediocrity reveals not the exhaustion of their attributes but the limits of our perception. To condemn our circumstantial world as dull and ugly is really to confess our own limited vision.

For all our tempering, cynical experience of the world we are linked in spiritual kinship to Don Quixote. He stands as a superlative metaphor of both our undeniable frailties and necessary audacity. The world also exceeds our strength and our hopes. We too shall know defeat in one form or another; sooner or later in our unequal striving we discover our limitations and face our mortality. Yet the quixotic quest remains as humanly authentic as it is foolish to the earthbound mind. This physical realm is not enough. Upon its mere materiality we, too, build the ideal structures of art and faith, hope and heroism, altruism and ethics, so that our life, so fearfully limited, so natively trivial, may transcend its circumscribed reality and point us toward truth, love, justice, grace, and beauty. The enormous gap between Don Quixote's anemic physical prowess and his heroic resolve reminds us of the long journey from who we are to who we would become.

But we must not be too hasty or go too far in claiming this metaphysical likeness. For unlike Don Quixote, we usually stop short in our commitments to justice, truth, and beauty, allowing common sense to bind us umbilically to our common world. For all our professed loyalty to the ideal, we do not trust it entirely or embrace it wholeheartedly. A measure of final prudence checks our heroism; at the moment of supreme truth and trial we are disquieted by second thoughts and tempted by easier alternatives. At the bottom of our heart stubborn doubt survives.

Don Quixote is uninfected by modern skepticism. For this reason, today few could summon such innocent determination in pursuit of a cause or commit themselves so radically to a quest in the first place. For the modern world frowns on mighty passion and dismisses as weakness the virtues it does not understand or possess. Mere equality has usurped the true mission of our humanism and in its name, we have deconstructed our formative myths and reduced heroism to the measure of our veniality. Modern heroes have become anti-heroes, champions of mediocrity and enemies of superiority, for modernity has defined itself as the cult of the common. Probably a contemporary Cervantes would invert the theme of the novel, deconstruct Don Quixote, and turn him into Alonso.

We began this section by asking how the Quixotic vision of life was related to the general understanding of human reality that Ortega and other Spanish thinkers have attempted to codify as a general human metaphysics. Let us see what answers are now possible.

If we can speak at all of a "Spanish" metaphysics, at least in the modern sense since Suárez, we must think in terms of a doctrine of human life and to imply at least a theory of personhood. Spanish concern for the abstract has always been a secondary matter, important only insofar as it claims a relationship to the personal. From their earliest history, the Spanish had always concentrated on anthropomorphic reality in their thinking. From Gracián to Unamuno this tendency grew more intense, and since Ortega it has achieved formal status of doctrine as well. It seems accurate to say that philosophical creativity in modern Spain appears in almost measurable ratio to how close or how far thinkers have stood in relation to the informing theme of human reality. In this regard, the thinkers of the several generations of 1898 revived and reinvigorated the foundational ideal of the West: the vision of human life as a special, radical, and created reality irreducible to no other condition or thing. Furthermore, Ortega's discovery of truth as **aletheia**, that is, as the revelatory and redemptive unveiling of truth is a phenomenon that occurs only in human, or better, personal life. **From this perspective, life, and especially Quixotic life, can thus be understood as the living, experiential manifestation of <u>aletheia</u>.**

We are tempted to define this uniqueness with modern democratic clichés—human freedoms, rights, moral responsibility etc.—but we come closer to the Spanish understanding when we realize that it is not primarily a matter of identifying abstract human qualities, not even the desirable ones, but of respecting at a deeper level the indivisible and invulnerable integrity of the individual person.

In summary, Spanish metaphysics, implicit in a line of thinkers, writers, and artists from Jorge Manrique to Gracián, Quevedo, Cervantes, and Unamuno, becomes an explicit philosophical doctrine of human life in Ortegan thought. It is the "radical reality" within which all realities appear in circumstantial relevance to us. Only in our life perspective do things reveal their hierarchical significances. And this means that the most urgent task of life—and philosophy—is not the esoteric problems of contemporary logic and linguistics, any more than it was in older philosophies the pursuit of conscience, essence, or things-in-themselves. Instead, it is the revelation, the **aletheia,** of things in their relationships to the human person in its two modes: men and women. Here the age-old circle of philosophical thought begins finally to close. Once again, as it was in the ancient days of Greece, mankind becomes the measure of things. After a long fascination with abstract constructions we are launched, as though from a new field of Ontígola, on the adventure of the human person.

F WHITHER ESPAÑA ?

Keeping in mind what we have said about the Quixotic vision of life, let us allow Unamuno to introduce our final theme: "The philosophy in the soul of my people seems to me to be the expression of an inner tragedy analogous to the tragedy in the soul of Don Quixote, the manifestation of a struggle between what the world as scientific reason reveals it to us, and what we wish it to be according to the teaching of our religious faith." [10] I have no interest here in revisiting the old quarrel between science and faith, even less the rift between reason and irrationality as Unamuno understood these themes. Nor need we do so after Ortega's rebuttal in <u>Meditations on Quixote</u>.

Yet if Unamuno was on shaky ground in drawing his conclusions, he was on much more solid footing in his assumptions. For he put his finger in the wound that Spain had suffered for many generations. During the seventeenth and eighteenth centuries, as much of Europe embraced successively religious schism, nationalism, and scientific skepticism, Spain found herself increasingly isolated. If the Spanish themselves were unsure of the road to take, they were at least certain Europe had taken the wrong one.

The resulting state of affairs was evident most of all to Spaniards themselves: Spain lost its transitive, active character. By refusing to go along, it ended up going nowhere. Spanish life, always surprisingly intense, spontaneous, and creative at the personal level, collectively was decidedly inferior to what the Spanish knew it ought to be. They watched the rest of Europe succeed with a dubious ideal, while they sensed their own failure to pursue a more exalted one.

It was to be an age of separations. In the nineteenth century Spain was separated from the Americas, or to say it better and more accurately, the Americas separated from Spain and from one another. But we must not think of this parting merely in political terms. In both Europe and the Americas the Hispanic world lost touch with its roots. Political separation was the consequence not the cause of a deeper estrangement. The outcome was predictable: in both hemispheres there occurred a series of identity crises that have lasted to this day, especially in the Americas. Ortega's cry, My God, what is Spain?, continues to echo in one form or another and varying intensity from Mexico to the Straits of Magellan. <u>Las Españas</u> (The Spains), probably Spain's greatest creation, disintegrated, and each part, including Spain itself, bravely declaring itself to be a self-sufficient whole, by its professed uncertainties, imitative proclivities, and much debated lack of direction indirectly confessed in each case that it was a part cast adrift. On both sides of the Atlantic Spanish-speaking peoples lost contact with their past, and since life is projected from its history, they also lost touch with their future.

In the case of Spain, this temporally localized or "cystic" incongruence was commonly but mistakenly interpreted as an entire history of incoherence. A sinister verdict was then rendered: both Spain and its offspring civilizations were afflicted by an incurable genetic disorder that could well doom them forever to chaos and disorder.

This assumption, often repeated by other nations and generally accepted intellectually and politically by Hispanic peoples themselves, gave rise to another with even more serious consequences. At those several crucial junctures where Spain deviated from Europe it was taken for granted that Spain was in error and Europe was in the right. Until Hitler and the Holocaust, European history tended to be interpreted deterministically. What happened historically was simply taken to be what had to happen. War, conquest, devastation, and defeat formed the unquestioned historical tapestry of Europe, and it would make no more sense to pass moral judgment on the course of events than it would to moralize about mountains and forests in a landscape.

Spanish history continues to be judged by a very different standard. For not only has Spain long stood accused for its actual history but even held morally accountable for an alternate history that never occurred.

The intellectual and moral oddity of this dual standard is obvious, but that observation is incidental to a more important one. When the same norms are applied to both histories, then not only the accusations against Spain but also the unquestioned assumptions about Europe become fair targets for our scrutiny. If, for example, we insist on speaking of Spanish "errors," then we must first understand our terms. When we speak of Spain's mistakes, do we mean its occasional departures and lapses from the internal and informing Spanish will to be Western, Christian, and eventually trans-European, or is our judgment rooted in various extraneous assumptions, e.g., that Spain "ought" to have accepted an Oriental and Islamic destiny, or that it should have confined itself to an intra-European role like, say, Austria or Sweden? Can we chide Spain, as Bacon did, for its opposition to the Protestant Reformation? Was it morally at fault because it did not see things from an English, Lutheran, or Calvinist point of view? Would we not hold Spain to a strange historical logic to expect the same society that had defended Catholicism as its very essence for over a thousand years to turn suddenly against it?

If we dismiss the notion of historical inevitability, which is alien to history, then Europe and the West become subject to similar questions and the possibility of similar mistakes. We can now wonder more insistently, picking up where we left off in an earlier chapter, whether European civilization erred in embracing the substitutionary idealism popularized by the Enlightenment *philosophes* and their intellectual heirs of more recent times. Was it a mistake to abandon the unique Christian vision of man and pledge allegiance instead to an animalistic and primitive theory of human life?

Today we speak glibly of the "post-Christian age," assuming as fact what we have yet to prove as possibility. For as far as I know, history offers no precedent, at least no successful one, of a people able to flourish after losing the defining trait that elevated them to greatness. Few peoples have a second chance in history. The Roman without sustaining virtue, the American or Englishman without gainful enterprise, the Spaniard without passionate faith, all stand in danger of becoming an accusing mockery of who they once were.

We are confronted by haunting, hypothetical alternatives to our historical past. If Christianity, which had always sponsored learning and knowledge, had not been traumatized, rent by suspicion and rancor, and put on the defensive by the Reformation, could it have given us a more humane and inclusive science? Are we condemned forever to a dehumanized science that refuses a priori to acknowledge the spiritual and denies the possibility of the transcendent? It is a poor science indeed that gives an answer without examining the evidence.

Throughout this book we have seen from different perspectives how the Spanish have clung tenaciously to an understanding of man as a person. And we have examined as well, their penchant for what I have called "concrete imagination," which we may sum up as a genius for the real. What if instead of turning its back when Europe embarked on its long ideological journey toward the abstract deconstruction of the human person, Spain had remained on the European scene to counter, to object, to offer alternatives? Who knows how many problems Spain—and perhaps the West—could have avoided or resolved if it had remained open to science. We spoke earlier of Spanish errors, and the evidence is overwhelming that in rejecting the good so as to avoid the evils inherent in modern culture, Spain committed a series of mistakes of immense, immeasurable proportions.

But here we must turn from regrets about the past and ask—as I asked my teachers long ago—what relevance Spain may still have in today's world? Materially speaking, Spain continues to be a country of relatively modest means, evidently better off than in times past but not yet up to the economic level of several other Western nations. Marginalized in earlier centuries and ostracized during much of the twentieth, until very recent decades Spain did not enjoy the technological advances experienced elsewhere in the West. Yet in its estrangement from modernity Spain was able to preserve in purer and more recoverable form the humanistic truths of the Classical and Judeo-Christian heritage of the West. For this reason, our inquiry about Spanish relevance leads us to an area that would surprise most Westerners. Early in the twentieth century, Spanish thinkers began to develop a philosophy centered on the radicality and uniqueness of human life that as far as I have been able to determine is unrivaled in the Western world. Compared to Ortega and Marías and the line of thought they represent, nearly all other philosophies of our time—deconstructionism, postmodernism, and varieties of neo-Marxism, among others—strike us as dull, unrewarding exercises in spiritual and intellectual futility.

But the germ of Ortegan/Marías doctrine is not confined to Spain. In the deepest sense this understanding of reality arises from the very heart of the Western tradition itself, and more particularly from the unique understanding of man on which the West was built. Hence the odd way it resonates in Western life, as I pointed out in the introductory chapter. Not by accident attempts to abandon this tradition have coincided with the celebrated crisis of modernity. There is a great deal of talk about replacing the older idealism, especially its Christian foundation, with more compatible concepts. But what might these be? The depth and duration of the crisis instead seem to underscore the shallowness of the new substitutionary ideals, not the insufficiency of the old. This is why today's celebrated "postmodernism" will likely prove to be not a revolutionary leap forward but a reactionary tumble into ancient errors.

For two thousand years the spirit of Spain has expressed itself in the invulnerable dignity and immortal worth of personal life. On these principles hang all its abiding art, literature, philosophy, ethics, religion, and governance. Only in moments of disorientation and doubt has it turned half-heartedly to the dehumanizing philosophies, debasing collectivism, and Machiavellian statism of modernity. And no sooner has it entertained these notions than it has rejected them. Even at its lowest moments, it has preferred to wander adrift to navigating by false coordinates.

Contrary to conventional views, throughout these many centuries Spanish history has been a tale of remarkable consistency and continuity. For all its lapses and moments of discouragement, Spain has never been without prophetic, enlightened voices calling on it to return to its abandoned destiny.

The spirit of Spain seemed to me to be an example worth considering and a tale worth telling. For as I said at the beginning, the story of Spain is also about those who share a common Western heritage by direct lineage, or in our day, by adoption.

The story is far from over. For the future is always the final dimension of history. But of this I shall say no more, not because there is nothing more to add but because these further chapters are a tale that only the Spanish themselves can tell.

Notes

CHAPTER I

1. I have observed that this Spanish familiarity with the departed differs in kind and degree from the generic "rule of the dead" in the Comtian sense as well as from what I would call "canonical reverence" for famous individuals of past eras conrn1on to all cultures. Shakespeare would be an object of the latter, and to the degree to which these figures loom larger than life, they rise above life, becoming immortal icons at the cost, naturally, of their human mortality. Today no one questions Shakespeare, except at the risk of playing the fool, for he has moved into a consecrated realm beyond the reach of our opinions and dislikes. To cast doubts on his genius would be the equivalent of arguing that the world is flat. With all the exceptions one may wish, the Spanish exhibit a very different attitude toward their famous dead. Instead of standing apart from everyday life, the latter continue to partake of it, ethereally rubbing shoulder to shoulder with ordinary people, still provoking loyalties and enmities. In other words, in Spain the departed do not soon depart from the stream of life. Instead, their personal space and individuality and their role in the running debates of life continue to be respected long after their physical demise.

2. <u>Politics and the Military in Modern Spain</u>, p. 1. Payne goes on to point out what he calls Spain's "religious decline" in modern times brought about by the encroachments of rationalistic thought in the spiritual domain of the Church. This aspect of Spain's so-called "decadence" needs more study.

3. Obras reunidas, p. 269.
4. Del sentimiento trágico de la vida, p. 236.
5. Julián Juderias, La leyenda negra y la verdad histórica. 6
6. I have studied these and other theories of Ortega in my early book José Ortega y Gasset: Philosopher of European Unity (1971). See especially the chapter entitled "Medieval Europe." This work was published in Spanish by Revista de Occidente (José Ortega y Gasset, filósofo de la unidad europea (1977).

7: Idearium Español, p. 73.

8: Julien Benda, El espíritu europeo. Both Benda and Ortega saw the desertion or betrayal of European *clercs* [intellectuals] as a relatively recent phenomenon. For others, however, it was the culmination of a long historical process. In Out of Revolution historian Eugen Rosenstock-Huessy speaks (unconvincingly, it should be added) of a five-hundred-year-old revolution by Europe's intellectual guardians.

9: To the hackneyed political and economic factors trotted out as the basis for the American and British assumption of Hispanic inferiority, it may be necessary to add another of which English speakers would scarcely have any awareness at all. I refer to ce1tain idioms of the English language itself. In English, and perhaps more so in the North American variety, it is customarily to refer to geographical movement south with the word "down." Thus one says, "I am going down south." In other words, the south—Mexico, Latin America, Africa, Spain, great portions of Asia, even the American South—to English speakers unconsciously becomes associated with the inferior, the lower; to go south (itself an idiomatic expression that indicates loss or an unlucky tum of events) is to descend to a lower level. It is as though the south were located physically and morally under the north, and all too often the English speaker behaves accordingly. Hence the "ugly American" of the postwar decades whose morality seemed to descend with the latitudes. On the other hand, the corresponding English-language idioms referring to the north substitute the word up (I am going up north, etc.) Unlike other European languages, English unwittingly imposes a certain prior scale of values on places merely because of their geography. North is the top and south is the bottom. In passing, I suggest that a subtle but important dimension of the history of the American South has to do with this language-induced sensation of being "under" the North, that is, of living with the "phantom" weight of the North on its shoulders.

10: See España inteligible, pp. 245-259.

11: From selections included in Jeux et sapience du Moyen Age, pp. 725-858. See, respectively, pp. 735-37 and 750-51 for his comments on the sphericity of the earth and the relative sizes of the Sun, Moon, and planets.

12: See España inteligible, pp. 301-303.

13: The case of Galileo is particularly revealing primarily because of what it has concealed historically. The perception that the Church waged a bitter war against science turns out to be for the most part another modern falsehood intended to discredit the Church. The Church itself had long encouraged science. In his book, The Sun in the Church, John L. Heilbron notes that it adapted cathedrals across Europe—Rome, Paris, Milan, Florence, Bologna, Brussels, and Antwerp—and constructed a tower in the Vatican itself for astronomical observations. As for Galileo, he was initially encouraged by the Church in his scientific studies and befriended by Catholic leaders. It was only after his petulance had outraged and estranged his former allies that he was brought to trial not primarily because of his science but his arrogance.

14: Bernadino de Sahagún,111, <u>Historia general de las cosas de Nueva España</u> . Bernal Díaz de! Castillo, <u>Verdadera historia de los sucesos de la conquista de la Nueva España</u>.

15: "Defensa de Espana," <u>Hispanoamérica vista por sus ensayistas,</u> p. 38 (my translation).

16: <u>Ibid</u>. p. 41 (my translation).

17: See his book <u>Literatura y generaciones,</u> pp. 221-242.

18: The popular anguish over the supposed overpopulation of the world and depletion of our finite resources seems to me to be naive and fraught with dangerous conclusions. In the end the fear reveals not the exhaustion of our resources but the exhaustion of our imagination and a dimming of our vision. The problem is not too many people but too little humanity, that is, too little trust in the very qualities—altruistic faith, artistic and technological creativity, ethics, and law—that set man apart from nature. The modern haste to restore man to nature is really a revolt against humanity and a repudiation of the age—old human struggle to escape the brutal terrors and savage brevity of natural life. Those who worship nature risk becoming reenslaved by it.

19: Bullfinch declares: "The Crusades were the mightiest, or rather, the most ambitious undertaking of the chivalry of Europe" (<u>The Age of Chivalry,</u> p. 250).

CHAPTER 2

1. "Prólogo para franceses," p. 116 [my translation]. This introduction to The Revolt of the Masses is not included in the sanctioned English translation of the work.

2: In a book alluded to earlier, José Ortega y Gasset: Philosopher of European Unity, I have studied Ortega's ideas on the original unity of Europe as well as an ideal of a future united Europe.

3: John Naisbitt (Megatrends, 2000) has argued that in ancient and medieval times men inherited their technology and therefore lived in the past. The Industrial Revolution abolished this dependence on the past and required men to master the technologies of the present. In recent times, however, not even the present suffices. Technology must be not only mastered but also anticipated. Hence post-modern man has begun to live in the future.

4: Y pues vos, claro varón,
    tanta sangre derramastes de paganos,
    Esperad el galardón
    que en este mundo ganastes por las manos;
English version of the Coplas by Thomas Walsh in Hispanic Anthology (1920).

5: Mysticism and Logic, p. 54.

6: En el mandato de Carlos V hay una lección del sentido ético del governante, que es lo que le diferencia de los demás mandatarios de Europa (Interview in La Vanguardia, July 30, 1999). I have discussed both the theme and the implications of the failure of *Universitas Christiana* in a paper delivered at the

Conference of European Studies, Omaha, October 1998.

7: See <u>España inteligible</u>, especially pp. I 07—119.

8: "On the True Greatness of Kingdoms and States," <u>The Philosophical Works of Francis Bacon</u>, p. 775.

9. <u>Erasmus and the Age of Reformation</u>, p. 113.

10: Erasmus, p. 111.

11: The Unfortunate Traveler and other Works, p. 479.

12: See Marías's illuminating discussion of these views in España inteligible, p. 145.

13: De rebus Hispaniae, Book IV, Ch. I.

14: See his Idearium Español, pp. 186 ff.

15: Al producirse la escisión, España se siente necesariamente vinculada a la Iglesia una por la cual había luchado con los musulmanes, hasta llegar a ser quien tenía que ser. La Reforma no era simplemente un movimiento crítico, ni siquiera una herejía dentro de la comunidad cristiana, sino un apartamiento, una ruptura; su aceptación por parte de España hubiera parecido, no sólo un pecado contra la fe, sino una infidelidad a la condición española, una deserción del larguísimo proyecto histórico en que se había realizado (España inteligible, p. 195).

16: España no ha peleado nunca por orgullo nacional, ni por orgullo de raza, sino por orgullo humano o por amor a Dios, que viene a ser lo mismo (Juan de Mairena, p. 102).

17: Economist Gonzalo Anes counters some of the common assumptions of Spanish decline by pointing out that even though rural Castile lost population during the sixteenth century, this was partially offset by an increase in urban areas. (Seville, for example, grew from a city of approximately 45,000 to 130,000 by the beginning of the seventeenth century.) Anes goes on to assert that throughout the reign of Philip 11 Castile was one of the most prosperous realms in Europe. See his article "La economía," "El mundo de Felipe II," Cuenta y Razón (Special Edition).

18: Lo que fue decisivo, y de efectos perdurables, fue el estado de ánimo de los españoles y de la mayoría de los extranjeros, en buena medida inducido en aquéllos por éstos. La impresión de decadencia quedó arraigada en las mentes y en las almas—justo al contrario de lo que sucedía desde el advenimiento de los Reyes Católicos hasta finales del XVI—; ni siquiera los hechos contrarios a la decadencia quebrantaban la convicción de su existencia e irreversibilidad ("Revisión de la Decadencia," España inteligible, p. 259).

19: Foolishness to the Greeks, p. 40.

20: In his book The Heretical Imperative Berger maintains that absent such uncontested beliefs and assumptions, there exists necessarily what he calls "the heretical imperative," that is, the personal, "heretical," and perhaps arbitrary decision by each Christian believer to be Christian, or to "believe" something else if he chooses.

21: Elle savait déjà peser les autorités, les comparer entre elles; elle a fini par les soumettre elles-mêmes au tribunal de la raison (Progrès de l'esprit humain).

22: The American Constitution alludes to God—given endowments—life, liberty, and the pursuit of happiness—and consists in a pledge to protect the inalienable gifts of the Creator. It is an attempt to wed the religious heritage of the Colonists to the rationalism of the Enlightenment.

23: <u>Foolishness to the Greeks</u>, p. 31.

24: <u>Human Knowledge and Metaphysics</u>, p. 190. He also describes (p. 11) the "imperialistic" stages of reason. There was a period of philosophical and metaphysical imperialism in the time of Plato and Aristotle; another of theological imperialism in the Middle Ages; and beginning with Descartes, Kant, and Comte, scientific imperialism has prevailed, resulting in a progressive descent of reason that has also per-mitted the modern technical mastery of materiality.

25: España, aunque ya estaba perdida toda esperanza en el éxito de su antiguo intento político, prefirió permanecer adormecida en el, sin fuerzas para crearse nuevos propósitos nacionales conforme a los nuevos tiempos que el desarrollo histórico de los pueblos trajo para Europa (See "Las dos Españas," Los españoles en la historia).

26: España inteligible, p. 162.

27: Foolishness to the Greeks, p. 41.

CHAPTER 3

1: Particularly in <u>A Watch over Mortality: The Philosophical Story of Julián Marías</u>, 1997.

2: <u>Historia de la lengua y literatura castellanas</u>. Cited by Luis Granjel in his study <u>La generación literaria del 98</u>, pp. 40-41.

3: "¿Cuántas de sus cualidades no han sido conscientes para los del 98 precisamente gracias a Ortega?" <u>Literatura Española contemporánea</u>, p.

4: <u>Obras completas</u>, III, p. 117.

5: Ortega gave some evidence of his opposition to the Unamunean notion of "tragic life" in the following commentary: "...from my first writings I have opposed the exclusivity of a 'tragic sense' as Unamuno bandied it about rhetorically with a 'spoliing and festive sense' of existence, which my readers, of course, understood in a purely literaly way" (<u>Obras completas</u>, III, p. 297) (as indicated elsewhere, translations are mine unless otherwise indicated).

6: La fenomenología no fue para nosotros una filosofía: fue una buena suerte (<u>Obras completas</u> VIII, p. 42).

7: La segunda generación...nace a la vida histórica y a la vida literaria cuando los hombres del 98 no están todavía en disposición de padrear a nadie. Su formación cultural, que es uno de sus caracteres decisivos, no debe nada a los hombres del 98, cuya influencia, por entonces, era casi nula (<u>Literatura española contemporánea</u>, p. 155).

8: Ortega writes: "Europa, cansada en Francia, agotada en Alemania, débil en Inglaterra, tendrá una nueva juventud bajo el sol poderoso de nuestra tierra".

España es una posibilidad europea.
Sólo mirada desde Europa es posible España"
(Obras completas, I, p. 138).

9: Generaciones y constelaciones, p. 273.

10: Se radicalizaron...las pretensiones de sus antecesores...Los hombres nuevos traerán a la política igual actitud que a la ciencia o al arte... Razón pura en la ciencia, en la política, y casi me atrevería a decir pureza racional e irracional en poesía (Cinco aventuras españolas, pp. 20-21.)

11...esta generación comienza proclamándose minoritaria: admite, desde un principio, la existencia de formas populares de arte, que rechaza por vulgares e indignas (Literatura española contemporánea, p. 166).

12: Esta generación, comparada con las demás de nuestro tiempo, muestra un predominio de las facilidades sobre las dificultades...Las hadas madrinas han solido acompañar fielmente al equipo de la generación de 1901 ("¿Generación de 1927?" Generaciones y constelaciones, p. 274).

13: Jacques Maritain has written with great insight about the "new Machiavellianism," the guiding assumption of modern totalitarianism that has inverted the classical concepts of ethics and morality. If peace is health and public wellbeing the aim of the Aristotelian and Classical republic, war and absolute power are, respectively, their totalitarian replacements. See "The End of Machiavellianism," The Range of Reason, pp. 134-164.

14: Hemos sentido que en ello iba la vida futura de España y la salvación de todo lo que nos parecía valioso, estimable, original, insustituible en un milenio de vida española, en medio milenio de creación universal, transespañola ("¿Generación de 1927?" Generaciones y constelaciones, p. 276).

CHAPTER 5

1. María Zambrano states: "Wise stoicism has in fact expressed the lay side of our culture and almost exclusively its philosophical thought... When the Spaniard has not lived within a religion, inevitably he has come to be stoic" ("El estoicismo español," Obras reunidas, p. 301).

2. Rousseau and Revolution, p. 80.

3. In the 1970's any number of academic and government "experts" (often the same people) in the United States were busily predicting—in some cases we may suspect with self-serving or ideological motives—that the entire South American continent would soon be divided between communist and military dictatorships and that economic ruin was only a matter of time. Fortunately, these predictions were wrong. Less fortunate is that most of these so-called experts were never held accountable for their mistakes.

4. This is not intended to be a simple play on words. I suspect that the germ of a Christian sociology, and probably other dimensions of knowledge, including a non-Hellenistic foundation for philosophy, is implicit in the Logos, which so far we have tried to understand only in theological terms. Naturally this is not the place to pursue this fascinating but boundless topic.

5. Gustave Flaubert, Correspondance, II, p. 305.

6. Ángel Ganivet attributes this duality of characters to Arabic and Semitic influence. Without it, he writes,"... [ellos] hubieran sido siempre un solo hombre, remedo de Ulíses [(they) would have been a single man, in imitation of Ulysses] (Ideárium, p. 304).

7. Possibly I am being too hasty in predicting how Don Quixote and Sancho would fare outside of Spain. Denis Diderot notes in <u>Jacques le fataliste</u> that Jacques and his Master are much diminished when separated,"...like Don Quixote without Sancho..." (p. 53).

8. Agustín Durán, for example, noted in his "Critica y teoría del romanticismo" [Critique and Theory of Romanticism] that "El objeto que el poeta se propone describir...no es ciertamente al hombre abstracto y exterior; es, si, al individual e interior..." [The object that the poet proposes to describe is certainly not the abstract, external man; it is, rather, the individual, inner man]. Cited in <u>Antología general de la literatura española</u>. II, pp. 123-4.

9. Si supiéramos con evidencia en que consiste el estilo de Cervantes, la manera cervantina de acercarse a las cosas, lo tendríamos todo logrado. Porque en estas cimas espirituales reina inquebrantable solidaridad y un estilo poético lleva consigo una filosofía y una moral, una ciencia y una política" (<u>Obras completas</u>, I, p. 163).

10. Aparecéseme la filosofía en el alma de mi pueblo como la expresión de una tragedia intima análoga a la tragedia del alma de Don Quijote, como la expresión de una lucha entre lo que el mundo es, según la razón de la ciencia nos lo muestra, y lo que queremos que sea, según la fe de nuestra religión nos lo dice" (<u>Del sentimiento trágico</u>, p 21).

Bibliography

Selected Works Cited or Consulted

Azorín (Martínez Ruiz). <u>Antonio Azorín</u>. Madrid: Biblioteca Nueva, 1939.

Balfour, Sebastian. <u>The End of the Spanish Empire, 1898-1923</u>. Oxford: Clarendon Press, 1967.

Baroja, Pío. <u>El árbol de la ciencia</u>. Madrid: Alianza Editorial, 1967.

Benda, Julien, et al. <u>El espiritu europeo</u>. Translated by M. Riaza. Madrid: Guadarrama, 1957.

Castro Américo. <u>The Spaniards: An Introduction to their History</u>. Berkeley and Los Angeles: University of California Press, 1954.

Chevalier, Tracy, Editor. <u>Encyclopedia of the Essay</u>. Chicago: Fitsroy Dearborn Publishers. 1997.

Durant, Will and Ariel. <u>Rousseau and Revolution (The Story of Civilization)</u>. New York: Simon & Schuster, 1983.

Flaubert, Gustave. <u>Correspondance</u>, II. Paris: Le Seuil, 1963.

Fox, E. Inman. <u>Meditaciones sobre la literatura y el arte</u>. Madrid: Castalia, 1987.

Ganivet, Ángel. <u>Obras completas</u>. 2 vols. Madrid: Aguilar, 1961.

García Morente, Manuel. <u>Idea de la hispanidad</u>. Madrid: Espasa-Calpe, 1961.

Gray, Rockwell. <u>The Imperative of Modernity: An Intellectual Biography of José Ortega y Gasset.</u> Berkeley: University of California Press, 1989.

Hegel, Georg Wilhelm Friedrich. Reason in History. Translated by Robert S. Hartman. Indianapolis-New York: Bobbs-Merrill Company, Inc., 1953.

Huizinga, Johan. Erasmus and the Age of Reformation. New York: Halver & Brothers, 1957.

Kamen, Henry Arthur F. The Spanish Inquisition: A Historical Revision. Press, New Haven: Yale University 1998.

Laín Entralgo, Pedro. ¿A qué llamamos España? Madrid: Espasa- Calpe, 1970.

_____. La generación del noventa y ocho. Madrid: Espasa-Calpe, 1983.

López-Morillas, Juan. Hacia el 98: literatura, sociedad, ideología. Barcelona: Editorial Ariel, 1972.

MacIntyre, Alisclair. After Virtue: A Study in Moral Theory. South Bend: Notre Dame Press, 1997.

Madariaga, Salvador de. Guía del lector del Quijote. Buenos Aires: Editorial Sudamericana, 1967.

Marías, Julián. España inteligible: razón histórica de las Españas. Madrid: Alianza Universidad, 1985.

Generaciones y constelaciones. Madrid: Alianza Editorial, 1989.

Maritain, Jacques. The Range of Reason. New York: Charles Scribener's Sons, 1952.

Menéndez Pidal, Ramón. El Padre las Casas: su doble personalidad. Madrid: Espasa-Calpe, 1963.

Nashe, Thomas. The Unfortunate Traveler and Other Works. London: Penguin Books, 1971.

Newbigin, Lesslie. Foolishness to the Greeks. Grand Rapids, Michigan: William B Erdmans Publishing Co. 1986.

Ortega y Gasset, José. <u>Obras completas</u>. 11 vols. Madrid: Revista de Occidente, 1961-69.

Payne, Stanley G. <u>Politics and the Military in Modern Spain</u>. Stanford University Press, 1967.

Rosenstock-Huessy, Eugen. <u>Out of Revolution. Autobiography of Western Man</u>. Norwich, Connecticut: Argo Books, 1969.

Sachar, Howard M. <u>Farewell España: The World of the Sephardim Remembered</u>. New York: Alfred A. Knopf, 1994.

Sahagún, Fr. Bernardino de. <u>Historia general de las cosas de Nueva España</u>. Mexico City: Editorial Porrúa, 1927.

Shaw, Donald. <u>The Generation of 1898 in Spain</u>. London: Earnest Blenn Limited, 1975.

Stradling. R. A<u>. Europa y el declive de la estructura imperial Española 1580-1720</u>. Translated by Jesús Fernández Sulaica. Madrid: Ecliciones Cátedra, 1992.

Torrente Ballester, Gonzalo. <u>Literatura española contemporánea</u>. Madrid: Afrodisio Aguado, 1949.

Tovar, A. y Blázquez, J. M. <u>Historia de la Hispania romana</u>. Madrid: Alianza Editorial, 1997.

Unamuno y Jugo, Miguel. <u>Ensayos</u>. 2 vols. Madrid: Aguilar, 1958.

Zambrano, María. <u>Obras reunidas</u>. Madrid: Aguilar, 1969.

Title: *Radical and Empirical Reality: Selected Writings on the Philosophy of José Ortega y Gasset and Julián Marías*
- Harold Raley
- Paperback: 276 Pages
- ISBN: 9781648830167
- Totalrecall Publications, Inc.

The essays and lectures that comprise this book reflect decades of work in the United States, Spain, and Spanish America. In no particular chronological sequence, these writings cluster in thematic unity around the innovative concepts of the shared vision of philosophers Ortega y Gasset and Julián Marías. These include, among others, human life as the radical reality, the indissoluble bond of person and circumstance, innovations of philosophic genre and lexicon, perspective as reality and history as reason, and beyond the reductive claims of modern biologism, realism, and idealism the unique reality of the human person as creation.

Review

Highly recommended for anyone interested in Ortega, Marias and vital reason!

This collection of essays on the philosophy of Ortega y Gasset and Julian Marias is a perfect introduction! The essays are divided into those on Ortega and those about Marias, although the author considers the two of them in most of the texts. For me, this served as a starting point for Julian Marias (I hadn't read any of his texts) and, whilst I was already a fan of Ortega, I found that Raley does a great job os summarizing the idea of life as "radical reality".

It's probably worth pointing out that a lot of these essays are in Spanish.

Amazon Verified Purchase
Reviewed in the United Kingdom GB on November 19, 2020

Title: *A Watch over Mortality*
- Harold Raley
- Paperback: 302 pages
- ISBN-13: 9780791431542
- State University of New York Press

A Watch over Mortality: The Philosophical Story of Julian Marias (Suny Series in Latin American and Iberian Thought and Culture)

In this book, Harold Raley offers the English-speaking world Julian Marias's compelling alternatives to contemporary minimalist thoughts, and does so in a dynamic style that itself reflects the humane spirit and verve of what may well prove to be the most innovative philosophy of modern times.

Reviews

"Well written and well thought out, this book brings us up to date on Marías by including the latest (and concluding) items in his substantial corpus of works. Author Harold Raley does for Marías what Marías tried to do for Ortega y Gasset, except that he does it better. He explicates, clarifies, justifies, and defines Marías's thought as a whole in the context of his life and his long-term relation to Ortega. His grasp of the issues is confident and convincing; his style is lucid and readable."

—John T. Graham, University of Missouri, Kansas City

"What I like most about this book is its lucidity, comprehensives, sympathy, and up-to-dateness. The problem-set dealt with Marias and the particular applications thereof, which are well presented and developed in context by the author, are right at the center of contemporary thought: rationalism vs. irrationalism, phenomenology and existentialism, feminism, etc. It identifies possible or alternative ways of examining and resolving these questions by faithful descriptive analysis and radicalization. The book has a novel-like quality which permits the author to write with style and achieve moments of depth and nonsuperfluous elegance."

-- Jorge Garcia-Gomez, Long Island University

www.ingramcontent.com/pod-product-compliance
Lightning Source LLC
Chambersburg PA
CBHW071959070526
44583CB00015B/1258